BECOMING a girl OF grace

a JOINT BIBLE STUDY
FOR TWEEN GIRLS and THEIR MOMS

♥ CATHERINE BIRD ♥

LEAFWOOD
PUBLISHERS
an imprint of Abilene Christian University Press

BECOMING A GIRL OF GRACE

LEAFWOOD
P U B L I S H E R S
an imprint of Abilene Christian University Press

Copyright 2017 by Catherine Bird

ISBN 978-0-89112-415-3

Printed in the United States of America

Leafwood Publishers is an imprint of Abilene Christian University Press
ACU Box 29138
Abilene, Texas 79699

1-877-816-4455
www.leafwoodpublishers.com

♥ Dedication ♥

For Dinora, one amazing girl of grace
who embraced every day as the gift it was.
I miss you, sweet friend.

*There are many virtuous
and capable women in the world,
but you surpass them all!*
Proverbs 31:29 (NLT)

CONTENTS

Acknowledgments vi
Introduction vii

♥ 1 ♥ **Girl of Grace Characteristic:** *Love* 1

♥ 2 ♥ **Girl of Grace Characteristic:** *Faith* 11

♥ 3 ♥ **Girl of Grace Characteristic:** *Wisdom* 21

♥ 4 ♥ **Girl of Grace Characteristic:** *Humility* 31

♥ 5 ♥ **Girl of Grace Characteristic:** *Courage* 41

♥ 6 ♥ **Girl of Grace Characteristic:** *Witnessing through* 53
          a Servant's Heart

♥ 7 ♥ **Girl of Grace Characteristic:** *Being a Godly Leader* 63

♥ 8 ♥ **Girl of Grace Characteristic:** *Accountability* 73

Facilitator's Guide

♥ 1 ♥ **Girl of Grace Characteristic:** *Love* 85

♥ 2 ♥ **Girl of Grace Characteristic:** *Faith* 91

♥ 3 ♥ **Girl of Grace Characteristic:** *Wisdom* 95

♥ 4 ♥ **Girl of Grace Characteristic:** *Humility* 99

♥ 5 ♥ **Girl of Grace Characteristic:** *Courage* 103

♥ 6 ♥ **Girl of Grace Characteristic:** *Witnessing through* 107
          a Servant's Heart

♥ 7 ♥ **Girl of Grace Characteristic:** *Being a Godly Leader* 111

♥ 8 ♥ **Girl of Grace Characteristic:** *Accountability* 115

About the Author 119

acknowledgments

This book would not have been possible without the love and support of my family, especially my wonderful husband. Travis, you are my heart. Thank you for your wisdom and all the laughter—even if it was often at my expense. You are such a godly man, and I thank God daily for the gift of you.

Thank you to the lovely moms and daughters who piloted the content of this study. What fun we had! Your friendships are sweet blessings that my daughters and I continue to cherish.

Rev. Katie Meek, there are simply no words to adequately express what a gift you have been to the development of *Becoming a Girl of Grace*. Thank you for your mentorship, your support, and most importantly, your friendship. You are the ultimate girl of grace!

My prayer warrior friends, who are too many to name—you know who you are. Thank you for your prayers and constant cheering. And thank you for loving me even when I disappeared into my writing hole. I love you all.

Dave and Laura, thank you for your guidance and advice. You are both proof that God has a grand design, and his plan is better than ours. You are beautiful people, and I feel blessed to call you friends.

Shari, my sweet sister in Christ, your love and support is too precious to put into words. Thank you for believing in this project, sharing my excitement and lending your time and talents to the development of this book design. You are awesome!

To my beautiful daughters, Ashley and Emma Kathryn, you are both the inspiration for the creation of this study. I love how close we are and that we aren't afraid to be silly. Always remember how much you are loved, and you are—deeply!

introduction

The purpose of *Becoming a Girl of Grace* is to take a closer look at some of the amazing ladies of the Bible and the character traits they model for modern tween girls. These women of yesterday have a lot to share with the girls of today! Coping with mean girls, feeling left out of a group of friends, learning to like yourself, and dealing with bullies are not new social dilemmas. The Bible is full of examples of strong females who chose to follow God and pursue faith despite what was happening in their world and cultures.

This study is prayerfully and intentionally written for tween girls to share with their moms. God made each and every one of us uniquely in his image. That means that while we are all created in his image, every single one of us is different and special in our own way. This includes moms and daughters. A mom and daughter may be part of the same family, but the inside of each person is special and unique. This study is a great way for tween girls and their moms to connect and share what is in their own hearts and minds!

explaining the Format of This study

Becoming a Girl of Grace is unique in that it is not broken down by daily reading and study. This is an eight-week-long study designed to facilitate joint Bible study and discussion between moms and daughters. Each week, we will examine a girl of grace character trait and discuss how women from the Bible modeled these characteristics for modern girls. This includes reading pertinent Scripture passages and thinking about how these excerpts from God's Word are relevant for girls today.

Moms and daughters may approach weekly study however it fits into their schedules. Read and study a little bit each day or consolidate into fewer days. This study is intentionally flexible. Daughters and moms may choose to answer the questions in each chapter together or on their own. If participating with a group, a facilitator can lead moms and daughters through some interesting discussions and fun activities that relate to each week's topic. A facilitator's guide is included in the back of this book to help with small group discussion. Facilitators will find discussion questions and activity ideas that correspond with each chapter.

mom and me activities

Another unique component of this Bible study is the "Mom and Me" weekly activity included in each chapter. These activities are meant to be enjoyable and inclusive for all family members. While this element of the Bible study is completely optional, it's sure to be entertaining! This can be an exciting adventure, so get started today and enjoy!

CHAPTER 1

girl of grace characteristic:

LOVE

Created Out of Love

Has anyone ever told you, "Wow, you look just like your mother!"? Or maybe someone has said to you, "I can see your father in you!" Genetics (which is the study of how traits are passed on from parent to child) is actually a pretty cool thing.

One of my favorite things to do as a young girl was sift through all of my family's old pictures. I would look at my baby picture, compare it to my brothers' baby pictures, and then compare those to photos of my mom and dad. There were even pictures of my grandmother and great-grandmother. My mom patiently answered tons of my questions like, "Who do people think you looked like when you were my age, Mom? Do I really have my grandmother's mouth? Why is my brother the only one in our family with blond hair?"

Have you ever wondered why you look the way you do? What about the way you act? Have you ever been told something like, "You inherited your dad's sense of humor" or "You have your grandmother's temper"?

Throughout this study, we're going to talk about the traits that can bring us closer to God and ultimately help us become girls of grace! Let's start with how we are made. You may get your baby-blue eyes from your mom, but your genetic code doesn't actually begin with your parents. It begins with God.

GOD'S PERFECT PLAN

Family is a gift. Whether your family is biological, adopted, or blended, God brought you together with love and purpose. Even though your brother or sister may not always feel like a joy, remember your heavenly Father carefully and lovingly crafted your family tree.

So God created human beings in his own image. In the image of God he created them; male and female he created them.

Genesis 1:27 (NLT)

The very first example we have of a girl of grace is evident in the creation of Eve. She was created out of love for love. Remember that Eve was created using one of Adam's ribs. God had a special purpose for her just as he has a special purpose for every single one of us. Eve was to be a helper, a wife, a friend, a mother, a cultivator, a caretaker, an encourager, and a leader.

Yes, yes—we know Eve made a big mistake when she took the forbidden fruit from the serpent in the garden of Eden but that doesn't change the loving purpose for which she was created. Like Eve, God created us out of love for love. We are created uniquely in God's image for a special purpose.

---

an activity for mom and me: GOD'S FAMILY TREE

* Find a good-sized twig (at least twelve to sixteen inches).

* Using clay in the bottom of a flower pot, stick the twig firmly into the clay.

* Cut out leaf shapes from construction paper (you can use green, yellow, red—whatever color you like!)

* Write as many family members' names as you can remember (use copies of photos if you like!). Each person gets his or her own leaf.

* Punch a hole at the bottom of the leaf and use string to tie the leaves to the twig.

NOTE: This is a great activity to learn more about your family history; but remember—at the top of your family tree is God!

♥ **Read Genesis 2:18–23.** Why do you think God chose to make Eve from one of Adam's ribs instead of making her from dust as he made all the other creatures of the world?

♥ Eve was created out of love for love. God has a loving purpose for you, too. Being young doesn't mean you have nothing to offer the world yet. Talk with your mom about the desires God has placed on your heart. What do you think it means for God to have a purpose for you? Jot some of your thoughts in the space below.

It is more blessed to give than to receive
Acts 20:35

Let's take a look at another example of love the Bible shares with us. One of my most favorite Bible stories growing up was the story of Naomi and Ruth. Talk about loving through difficult times! Naomi lost everything—her husband and both of her sons—and she was in a foreign land when all this happened.

Naomi and her husband, Elimelech, were Israelites who left Bethlehem—the promised land where people worshipped God. There was not enough food to eat because of a famine, and they had two boys to feed in addition to themselves. Can you imagine having to pick up and leave everything you know because there wasn't enough food to eat? Picture in your mind what it must be like to travel to another country with practically no possessions—just your family. And traveling would be rough! No airplanes, no cars, no iPod!

Well, that's what Naomi and her husband did. They moved with their sons, Mahlon and Kilion, to the country of Moab, a land where people worshipped false gods and idols. As if moving wasn't difficult enough, Naomi's husband died a short time after they moved to their new home. She was left to care for her two boys alone. Moms in those days didn't have great-paying jobs. There weren't play groups and social clubs where Naomi could meet other moms with little boys. Nonetheless, Mahlon and Kilion grew to be men and married Moabite women. Sadly, both of Naomi's sons died after living in Moab for about ten years.

Naomi was an outsider in a foreign country with no way to provide for herself. Envision how lonesome for home she must have been! Since the famine had ended in Israel, Naomi decided to return to her homeland

and birthplace. She and her daughters-in-law, Orpah and Ruth, packed their bags and prepared to hit the road for Judah.

But Naomi knew she could not care for her sons' wives. These women were from Moab, and the country Naomi was ready to leave was all these young girls knew. Can you fathom leaving your home? The only way of life you've ever known? Naomi knew this was too much to ask, so she blessed each daughter-in-law and asked them to return to their own families.

> Then Naomi said to her two daughters-in-law, "Go back, each of you, to your mother's home. May the LORD show you kindness, as you have shown kindness to your dead husbands and to me. May the LORD grant that each of you will find rest in the home of another husband." Then she kissed them good-by and they wept aloud and said to her, "We will go back with you to your people." But Naomi said, "Return home, my daughters. Why would you come with me? Am I going to have any more sons, who could become your husbands? Return home, my daughters; I am too old to have another husband. Even if I thought there was still hope for me—even if I had a husband tonight and then gave birth to sons—would you wait until they grew up? Would you remain unmarried for them? No, my daughters. It is more bitter for me than for you, because the LORD's hand has turned against me!"
>
> At this they wept aloud again. Then Orpah kissed her mother-in-law good-by, but Ruth clung to her.
>
> "Look," said Naomi, "your sister-in-law is going back to her people and her gods.
>
> Go back with her." But Ruth replied, "Don't urge me to leave you or to turn back from you. Where you go I will go, and where you stay I will stay. Your people will be my people and your God my God. Where you die I will die, and there I will be buried. May the LORD deal with me, be it ever so severely, if even death separates you and me."
>
> Ruth 1:8–17

Naomi tried to send her daughters back to their families, but they resisted. When Naomi was persistent, Orpah packed her bags and hit the road. But Ruth did not. Ruth lovingly followed Naomi to Bethlehem in the land of Judah. Even though she must have felt scared and unsure about leaving the only home she had ever known, she made that journey with great heart. Ruth wanted to care for Naomi, who had lost her husband and both of her sons.

Naomi and Ruth exhibit the girls of grace character trait love in the most selfless way. Naomi, who loved her daughters-in-law, sent them back to their families because she wanted them to be safe and happy. Ruth loved Naomi so deeply that she left her homeland. Ruth chose to worship Naomi's God over the false gods and idols she had been raised to believe in.

When Naomi and Ruth arrived in Bethlehem, the barley fields were ready for harvest. Ruth asked Naomi if she could go behind the harvesters to gather any leftover grain so that she and Naomi would have something to eat. The characteristic of love is also reflected in the service of stewardship and care. Both of these women cared for one another when they had nothing more to offer than love and loyalty.

♥ Naomi and Ruth both show us what it means to be a loving friend to family members. How can you take what you have read in their story

 girl of grace HEART CHECK

and apply it to your life today?

♥ Family relationships are important, but it's not always easy to share the best of yourself with the people who live under the same roof with you. Why do you think that is?

♥ Talk with your mom about what stewardship means to both of you. You may have different thoughts on what it means to love and care for something or someone. It's not the first time you and your mom will look at something from different points of view.

♥ Despite the differences you may encounter, what can you learn from Naomi and Ruth that can help strengthen the relationship between you and your mom?

What can you take away about love and stewardship? You may be young, but you have much to offer. God created each and every one of us with love and detail. We are unique, yet God's image is reflected in every single one of us. Your unique purpose may yet to be revealed to you, but rest assured, sweet friend: you are important to God's kingdom.

From a MOMMY'S HEART

Moms, what does it mean to love unconditionally? As young girls and not-so-young girls, we have all made choices that disappointed our parents at one time or another. I can remember one choice in particular that made me question if my parents would still love me the same as they did before I made that awful choice.

When I was a freshman in high school, I became good friends with another girl, who encouraged me to skip school and make choices that I knew in my heart didn't honor God, my parents, or me. I had a very happy childhood with loving parents who didn't talk with me about a lot of the activities that other kids my age found cool. Maybe it was because I was the youngest child and they thought I knew from watching my older brothers. Maybe it was because I was a girl, and they wanted to protect me. Maybe it was because they truly weren't aware of the potential for peer pressure. Regardless, I was unprepared to address the pressures of indulging in some of these activities—because ultimately, I cared a lot about what my friends thought of me.

In preparation for a fun night out, my friend and I arranged to spend the night at each other's houses. Translation—my parents thought I was staying at her house and her parents thought she was staying at mine. To make a long story short . . . we got caught. And afterward I remember being so relieved that I could talk with my parents about the events that had unfolded. I wanted my independence, but I needed the security of my parents' supervision as well. I didn't know how to ask for both.

I can still remember sitting in my parents' living room and listening to my dad as he said how disappointed he was in me. In that moment, I felt as though my parents didn't understand how I felt and would no longer be able to look at me and love me as they had the day before. That was a fallacy that Satan planted in my mind and that our world cultivates among our youth.

It simply wasn't true. My parents did still love me, and later I realized there was nothing I could do to ever change the way they felt. Parents are designed to love their children unconditionally. Since we are molded in God's image, this makes perfect sense.

Was God disappointed when Adam and Eve sinned? Yes! Did he punish them? Yes! Did he stop loving them? No!

The mother/daughter relationship is so unique and special. In today's world, so many external sources and temptations compete for our children's attention. No matter what age our daughters are, they are susceptible to hearing and believing that their mothers don't understand how they feel and don't care what they think.

It is important to me, as the mother of two daughters, to debunk the myths that the world tries to feed my girls. That is the purpose for creating this study—to help mothers and daughters strengthen their relationships through studying Scripture together. We may not always agree with our daughters, and that is absolutely okay. But we can instill in these sweet girls the confidence that their mothers will always be present with sympathetic ears, open minds, and loving hearts.

girl of grace characteristic:
FaITH

The power of Faith

Growing up, there was a game my friends and I loved to play. We would take turns holding out our arms, closing our eyes, and then falling backward with complete faith that someone would be behind us to catch us before we hit the ground. We trusted, even though we couldn't see, that unseen hands would keep us from falling and getting hurt. You may have tried this with your friends, too!

This is what it's like to have faith in God. Think about the air we breathe every day. You can't see it. You can't touch it. Yet, you have faith it is all around you.

Definition of *faith*:
firm belief in something for which there is no proof
—*Merriam-Webster Collegiate Dictionary*
www.merriam-webster.com

This week's girl of grace characteristic is faith. We are going to take a closer look at what it means to walk in faith . . . not just express what we believe with our words, but actually put our faith into action. The Bible is full of marvelous examples of faith, but we are going to examine four women in particular: Sarah (wife of Abraham), Mary (Jesus's mother), Elizabeth (John the Baptist's mother), and "the woman in the crowd." Each of these amazing women shares a story of faith with us and illustrates what happens when we put our complete trust in the Lord.

an unexpected Blessing

Sarai (later renamed Sarah by God), who we first meet in the book of Genesis (Genesis 11:29) was the wife of Abram (who God later renamed Abraham). They were a wealthy couple from the town of Ur. Imagine a busy city with lots of businesses, lots of people, and lots of money! Ur (which is now what we know as southern Iraq) was a pretty great place to live when Abram and Sarai were alive. They had wealth and all the comforts that come with being from a privileged class. The only dark spot in their wonderful life was Sarai's inability to have a baby of her own.

When Abram was in his sixties, God told him it was time to leave the big city for a place that would be revealed to Abram at a later time. So he and Sarai packed their belongings and left their home and all the luxuries the big city had to offer. They became nomads, which meant they camped a whole lot!

Think about how old your mom was when you were born. Now think about how old your grandmother was when you were born. Well, Sarah was even older than that when she began her pilgrimage away from Ur and eventually began to doubt she would ever be able to have a child. But God knew better!

When Sarai was ninety years old, she received a shocking message from God. She was going to have a baby! Did you catch that? She was ninety! This amazing woman of faith left her home when she was nearly sixty years old because she had faith in God's message for her husband, Abram. She was not only faithful to God, but she was faithful to her husband. God recognized her faith and blessed her with a child when she thought she was beyond the age to have a baby.

That baby's name was Isaac. With the promise of his birth and of many more family members to come, God blessed Abram and Sarai—giving them the names of Abraham and Sarah and promising that Sarah would be the mother of nations (Genesis 17:1–22).

Jesus's disciples later shared Sarah's story as an example of faith.

It was by faith that even Sarah was able to have a child, though she was barren and was too old. She believed that God would keep his promise.

Hebrews 11:11 (NLT)

girl of grace HEART CHECK

♥ **Read Genesis 12:1–9.** Pretend your mom tells you, "We are leaving our home. God has called us away for important work!" How would you feel? What would you pack? Could you pick up and leave everything behind as Sarah and Abraham did?

♥ **Read Genesis 18:10–14.** Having a baby when she was ninety years old was really funny to Sarah. Nothing is beyond God's power if we have faith. Can you think of a time when God answered one of your prayers in a very unexpected way? Mom, you share, too!

Because God Said So

Another woman who became a mom very late in life was John the Baptist's mom, Elizabeth. The Bible tells us that she and her husband, Zacharias, were well advanced in years when an angel of the Lord told them they would have a baby boy named John (see Luke 1:5–13). God recognized Elizabeth's faithfulness, and He rewarded her.

> *Blessed is she who has believed that the Lord would fulfill his promises to her!*
>
> Luke 1:45

an activity for mom and me: NOMADIC NOTIONS

Envision what it must have been like to pack up when there was no more food to eat, always sleeping in a tent or a cave. This is what it means to be a nomad. When Abraham and Sarah left the big city of Ur, they were choosing a completely new way of life.

Well, you and your mom are going to find out what nomadic life might have been like for Sarah and her family.

* Construct a tent house in your home somewhere. Maybe you can set up your tent in your bedroom or your living room. Make it as comfy as possible! Of course, you'll need pillows and your favorite blanket! Settle in with your mom (and maybe your dad and brother or sister). Nomads sometimes even slept under the stars when there was not enough room in the tent for everyone. Now, you realize . . . uh-oh. There's no food here. No berries. No animals to hunt. Nothing. Guess what? It's time to move.

* Pack up your tent, your pillow, and your favorite blanket and move everything to a new spot in the house. Don't forget baby sister if she's with you!

* Now, once you're all settled in your new location, you can relax. Moving is hard work! If Mom says it is okay, leave your tent in its current spot for a day or so. It's a great place for you to rest, read a book, eat a snack, and giggle with your mom.

* After a day or so, though, you realize that your new location just isn't working. There's not as much room as you first thought, and food is hard to find. There's no water. Oh, no. Guess what? It's time to move again!

* So pack up your tent once more. Grab your pillow and your blanket (and baby sister, too). Move your tent to another spot in your house. What a pain, right? Well, this is what life was like for nomads. They didn't know how long they would be in one place. Think about Sarah's faithfulness as she obeyed God's command to leave Ur!

Elizabeth's relative, Mary, was also visited by an angel of the Lord around the same time as Elizabeth. She was not yet married, but she was planning to marry a carpenter named Joseph. God sent the angel Gabriel to Mary to share news that she would give birth to the Son of God. Even though Mary must have been afraid, she submitted to God's will with simple acceptance (see Luke 1:38) because God said so!

Mary models what it is to believe in God without reservations and accept God's will. You may be thinking, "I'm a young girl! How can I understand what these old ladies and a girl from two thousand years ago were feeling and experiencing?" That's a good question.

The answer is, we can understand them because we know what it is to really, really want something in our own lives. Maybe it's a new bike. Maybe it's to pass that math test on Thursday! Maybe it's some other desire in your heart. We have the same feelings that Sarah, Elizabeth, and Mary did. They laughed just as we do. They shed tears and probably felt their share of hurt feelings and anger. They also each held desires in their hearts just as we do today.

And you know what? Our hearts' desires are just as important to God as the desires of these faithful ladies of the Bible who lived so long ago. God wants us to share our dreams and our fears with him. He wants us to lay them at his feet and trust him to handle them with care. God wants us to have faith that he knows what's best for us and will grant blessings in his time instead of ours.

Have you ever wished upon a star? I certainly have! My girls and I have held hands, stared at the sky, and made many wishes! I grew up believing that if you really, really believed something was possible, it could happen! Imagine having that kind of faith and confidence in God's plan for you!

Let's take a peek at a passage from Mark 5:21–36.

> Jesus got into the boat again and went back to the other side of the lake, where a large crowd gathered around him on the shore. Then a leader of the local synagogue, whose name was Jairus, arrived. When he saw Jesus, he fell at his feet, pleading fervently with him. "My little daughter is dying," he said. "Please come and lay your hands on her; heal her so she can live."
>
> Jesus went with him, and all the people followed,

crowding around him. A woman in the crowd had suffered for twelve years with constant bleeding.

She had suffered a great deal from many doctors, and over the years she had spent everything she had to pay them, but she had gotten no better. In fact, she had gotten worse. She had heard about Jesus, so she came up behind him through the crowd and touched his robe. For she thought to herself, "If I can just touch his robe, I will be healed." Immediately the bleeding stopped, and she could feel in her body that she had been healed of her terrible condition.

Jesus realized at once that healing power had gone out from him, so he turned around in the crowd and asked, "Who touched my robe?"

His disciples said to him, "Look at this crowd pressing around you. How can you ask, 'Who touched me?'"

But he kept on looking around to see who had done it. Then the frightened woman, trembling at the realization of what had happened to her, came and fell to her knees in front of him and told him what she had done. And he said to her, "Daughter, your faith has made you well. Go in peace. Your suffering is over."

While he was still speaking to her, messengers arrived from the home of Jairus, the leader of the synagogue. They told him, "Your daughter is dead. There's no use troubling the Teacher now."

But Jesus overheard them and said to Jairus, "Don't be afraid. Just have faith."

Mark 5:21–36 (NLT)

Oh, my goodness! Who likes to be sick? Can you conceive being sick for twelve long years, visiting doctor after doctor but having none of their medicines work? How terrible! Think about how you stay away from your friends when they are sick and how other people stay away from you when you are sick. This poor lady was probably no longer welcomed by any of her friends around town. She must have been very lonely! I get tired of staying in bed after a couple of days . . . it's tough to imagine being away from other people for days—much less years!

The woman in the crowd shows unbelievable faith. She thought, "If I can just touch the edge of Jesus's robe, I will be well." She didn't try to stop him or speak directly to him. She believed with all of her might that touching the fabric of his clothes would be enough. And it was!

What does Jesus say to her? He says, "Daughter, your faith has made you well. Go in peace. Your suffering is over." I included a couple more lines from this passage, because Jesus's original goal wasn't to heal the woman in the crowd. He was actually headed home with Jairus whose daughter was sick. Messengers arrived while Jesus was talking to the woman in the crowd and said not to bother him, because the young girl had died. But what did Jesus say? He said, "Don't be afraid. Just have faith."

 ## girl of grace HearT CHeCK

💗 These women of the Bible made a conscious choice to be faithful to God. That means they had to think about putting their commitment into action. How can you make faith a verb, and put yours into action? I bet you already are!

💗 Write your name, today's date, and the biggest wish in your heart on a piece of paper. Ask your mom to do the same. Put the papers in an envelope, and pray together as you give these desires to God. Now, put them in your family Bible and leave them there. It's neat to read these later to see how God moves in our lives! Remember, God's timing may not be yours!

> *Jesus looked at them intently and said, "Humanly speaking, it is impossible. But with God everything is possible."*
>
> Matthew 19:26 (NLT)

From a MOMMY'S HEART

Okay, we've all been there: the day when out of your mouth came the words of your mother. After a quick gasp, and perhaps a concerned look from your husband, you realize that you have just given a perfect impersonation of your own sweet mom. Oh, dear.

It's not your fault—really it's not! As children, we soak up the mannerisms and behaviors of our parents and caregivers. You've heard the cliché: "Monkey see, monkey do." Well, what happened to you the day you first uttered the words of your mother was mimicry at its finest.

Some of the traits we pass on to our children are unintentional, and some of those are fuel for material like National Lampoon's Christmas Vacation. We laugh, because there's a scary truth buried under all those punch lines!

But what about the intentional traits and legacies we want to pass to our little darlings? You can't control all the things that touch and influence your children, but you can absolutely be a part of that amazing concoction that will determine the adult your child becomes.

For me, the most important legacy I can pass to my girls is faith in God. Sadly, we live in a world that doesn't model faith for our children. Quite the contrary, our kiddos encounter obstacles to faith in this world every single day.

A dear friend of ours is gravely ill with stage 4 cancer. Her boys are the same ages as my girls and they have been in class together since kindergarten. Our friend has battled and beaten back breast cancer—twice!—only to be diagnosed less than a year later with stage 4 bone cancer. My girls don't understand. None of us understands! Yet, even with a broken heart, I hold my girls' hands and reaffirm my faith that God is sovereign and ever in control.

My girls may drive their husbands batty one day with some crazy quirk they get from their dear old mom, but I hope they also inherit a genuine faith that God is present. God is listening. God is always faithful.

> "I am reminded of your sincere faith, which first lived in your grandmother Lois and in your mother Eunice and, I am persuaded, now lives in you also."
>
> 2 Timothy 1:5

girl of grace characteristic:

WISDOM

a word to the wise

When you think of the word "wise," what comes to mind? What does it mean to have wisdom? Do you have to be smart to be wise? Do you have to be old to be wise? And just for fun, share with your mom what you consider to be old. Moms, try not to laugh or cringe or both!

When I think of examples of wisdom in the Bible, Solomon immediately comes to mind—of course! He is touted as the wisest man to have ever lived! The book of Proverbs is a wonderful resource on wisdom to be sure, but Solomon isn't our focus this week. Staying true to our girls of grace study, we are going to examine examples of wisdom as modeled for us by Miriam, Deborah, and Abigail. As you might have guessed, this week's girl of grace characteristic is wisdom.

Definition of wisdom:
a: accumulated philosophic or scientific learning : KNOWLEDGE
b: ability to discern inner qualities and relationships : INSIGHT
c: good sense : JUDGMENT
—*Merriam-Webster Collegiate Dictionary*
www.merriam-webster.com

Wisdom is kind of like knowledge, but it's different. Wisdom is similar to insight but not quite the same. Wisdom could easily be described as good judgment, but it's more than that. The definition of wisdom includes three key words: "knowledge," "insight," and "judgment." The combination of the three works to help a person make good choices.

Imagine walking into class at school one day. It's been a good day so far, and you just know it's only going to get better. Then, you walk into your classroom, find your seat, and gaze at the board as you prepare for class to begin. Oh, no! In bold letters on the board are the words, "Test today!" The problem? You forgot and didn't study. When your best gal pal realizes your dilemma, she assures you everything will be fine. She did study, and you can copy her work—no problem.

Stop. Now, you know the difference between right and wrong, but we don't always exercise wisdom and make the right choice. While the offer to copy your friend's answers might be tempting, the wise response would be something like, "Wow, Gina. You are so kind to offer, but I need to take whatever time I can and study now. No matter how I do on today's test, I won't let this happen again!"

Sometimes, we gain wisdom through knowledge and life experiences, but wisdom also comes from God. Miriam, Moses' big sister, models this beautifully for us! Let's look at Exodus 2:1–8.

> *Now a man of the tribe of Levi married a Levite woman, and she became pregnant and gave birth to a son. When she saw that he was a fine child, she hid him for three months. But when she could hide him no longer, she got a papyrus basket for him and coated it with tar and pitch. Then she placed the child in it and put it among the reeds along the bank of the Nile. His sister stood at a distance to see what would happen to him.*
>
> *Then Pharaoh's daughter went down to the Nile to bathe, and her attendants were walking along the riverbank. She saw the basket among the reeds and sent her female slave to get it. She opened it and saw the baby. He was crying, and she felt sorry for him. "This is one of the Hebrew babies," she said.*
>
> *Then his sister asked Pharaoh's daughter, "Shall I go and get one of the Hebrew women to nurse the baby for you?"*
>
> *"Yes, go," she answered. So the girl went and got the baby's mother.*
>
> Exodus 2:1–8

Miriam was a Hebrew living as a slave in Egypt. The pharaoh was a cruel man who ordered all Hebrew baby boys to be put to death when they were born. Jochebed, Moses' mother, wanted her baby to live, so she set him afloat in the reeds of the Nile River. Miriam watched her baby brother float down the river toward the spot where the pharaoh's daughter was bathing. When she overheard the sympathy that pharaoh's daughter had for Moses, she boldly stepped forward.

God gave Miriam the wisdom to ask if the pharaoh's daughter wanted her to fetch a wet nurse for the baby. When she was commanded to do so, Miriam retrieved her own mother! They were able to bring Moses home and raise him safely until he could return to the palace. His life was forever changed, and as we know, God used Moses to set the Israelites free from Egyptian slavery!

Miriam was just a young girl, but God gave her the wisdom to make an important choice that would forever change the lives of the Israelites. So do you have to be "old" to have wisdom? Definitely not! You are never too young to ask God for the wisdom to make a good choice when also faced with a potentially wrong one.

 girl of grace HearT CHECK

♥ Talk with your mom about what wisdom means to you. What is the difference between having knowledge and applying God's wisdom in our everyday lives? Give an example of a wise choice you've made recently and why you think it was wise.

💜 Who is the wisest person you know? Moms and daughters, take time for each of you to share your thoughts. Why do you think this person has such wisdom?

💜 If you were in Miriam's place, how would you have felt to watch your baby brother floating down the Nile River? Talk with your mom about how cultures may be different, but our choice to ask God for wisdom remains the same.

an activity for mom and me: SHOW ME THE WAY!

Do you know what a compass is? A compass is a tool used to help travelers find their way. The little instrument always points north, so the person holding the compass always knows which direction is north, south, east, or west. Applying wisdom is somewhat like having a compass inside of you. Your sense of right and wrong along with your life experiences help point you in the right direction when making a choice.

Does this mean we're never going to make a mistake? Sorry, but no. We all mess up from time to time. However, with God's help and our desire for wisdom, we can help keep our internal compasses in tip-top working order!

Now, it's time for you and your mom to make your own compass! Here is what you'll need:
- sewing needle
- small magnet or refrigerator magnet
- a small piece of cork (moms, about the size of a wine bottle cork)
- a small glass or cup of water

1. Rub the magnet over the needle fifty to sixty times in the same direction. Going the same direction is important. This magnetizes the needle.
2. Cut off a small circle from one end of the cork, about one-quarter inch thick. Lay the circle on a flat surface.
3. Carefully poke the needle into one edge of the circle and force the needle through the cork so that the end comes out the other side. Push the needle far enough through the cork so that about the same amount of needle is sticking out each side of the cork. Pliers are great for this.
4. Fill the glass or cup about half full of water, and put the cork and needle assembly on the surface of the water.
5. Place your "compass" on a flat surface and watch what happens. The needle should point toward the nearest magnetic pole—north or south, depending upon where you live.

Wisdom is More Than a Good Sense of Right and Wrong

When you have a disagreement with your friend, who helps you settle your differences? If you're fortunate, you are able to work out the problem yourselves. What about if you have an argument with your brother or sister? How do you resolve the fight in a fair and amicable way? You can't always settle conflict on your own. Sometimes, you need help. Maybe the person who helps you is your mom or dad, another sibling, or even a friend. Perhaps another adult wisely helps you see the problem from both sides.

Occasionally, we also need someone to keep us accountable. If your mom and dad didn't make you do your homework, would you be disciplined enough to do it every day? What about cleaning your room? No one is perfect, and we all need to be reminded from time to time about what's important.

The Israelites were no different. Their relationship with God is like our relationship with God. Sometimes we forget to talk to God about what's happening in our lives and ask him for guidance and help.

During biblical times, there was a period when the Israelites were led by judges instead of ruled by kings. We think of a judge as a person who works in a courtroom and helps resolve legal matters between two people. The leaders who are reflected in the book of Judges weren't so different from our view of judges today. However, they had a lot more responsibility!

One of the judges mentioned in the Bible is Deborah (see Judges 4:1–17 and 5:1–31), wife of Lappidoth—the only female judge named. She was well known for her wisdom and

KISS AND MAKE UP!

My brothers and I definitely didn't always see eye to eye when we were younger. My parents tried the normal dispute-settling tactics by saying things like, "Say you're sorry . . . Take turns please . . . Treat each other the way you want to be treated. "

However, one particular day, my dad stumbled onto what my brothers and I thought was the craziest idea ever! Whoever was arguing had to stand in a corner, hugging each other, and taking turns telling the other how much each was loved. Needless to say, after that particular treaty, peace was kept for quite some time! I think my dad was on to something!

Can you imagine having to trade compliments with the person who made you angry? Brilliant, Dad!

fairness. Many Israelites came from near and far to settle their disputes beneath the "Palm of Deborah."

Deborah was the recognized spiritual leader of the Hebrew people, but she wasn't a great military leader. The other judges were thought to have both skills, but this didn't bother Deborah or the people she led. Deborah was good buddies with a man named Barak, who was a great military leader. He depended on Deborah and the wisdom God gave her to lead them into battle against the great Canaanite military leader Sisera. God helped the Israelites defeat their enemy, and Deborah was celebrated for her wisdom.

abigail saves the Day!

Let's talk about Abigail, who was a just a normal girl from the wilderness of Maon. She was married to a shallow and selfish man named Nabal, a name which literally means "fool." Now, think about when someone comes to your house. Your family tries to make your guest feel welcome. That's called hospitality. In biblical times, hospitality was taken very seriously. It was considered a major insult not to welcome a stranger and offer him or her the best you had.

Well, as it so happens, David (yes, the future great king) was traveling through the land near Abigail's home. He and his troops rested on Nabal's land and, while they were there, they protected his shepherds during sheep-shearing season. When David asked for hospitality in return, Nabal said, "No way! Who does this David think he is?"

You can imagine how well this news was received. David was furious! He and his men set out to kill Nabal. When Abigail heard David was coming, she quickly packed fine gifts and met him on his way to her home. She bowed before him, accepted blame for any offense toward David, and apologized for her husband's rude behavior—reminding David that her husband was a fool, just as Nabal's name meant.

Read 1 Samuel 25:24–31. Through Abigail's actions, she prevented David from committing murder. He responded by praising God and complimenting Abigail on her wisdom!

> David replied to Abigail, "Praise the LORD, the God of Israel, who has sent you to meet me today! Thank God for your good sense!"
>
> 1 Samuel 25:32-33 (NLT)

So what does all this mean for a girl of grace today? We can take at least two things away from these ladies of long ago. The first thing is they asked God for wisdom and listened when he answered their prayers. Secondly, they applied that wisdom to their lives, which allowed God to work through them. What seemed like small events or split-second decisions (like Miriam) was actually God at work. He used those individual choices to do great things—like free a nation, repeatedly, and save a future king!

Imagine what God can do through you if you seek his wisdom and apply that wisdom to even the smallest choices in your life. Just because you're young doesn't mean God can't work through you, and it's never too early to start making the wise choice!

 ## girl of grace HearT CHeCK

* What would have happened if Miriam, Deborah, and Abigail hadn't used their wisdom? What do their actions tell us about what wisdom does to make our lives better?

* Talk with your mom about what it means to make wise choices in everyday life. Sometimes, our daily decisions seem insignificant, but they can also feel really important . . . such as using wisdom to choose friends or sharing wisdom in situations where others may not want to choose the path that honors God. How do you handle situations like this?

From a MOMMY'S HEART

"When you're a parent, you'll understand." How many of us heard this from our own parents when we were kids? I can remember being disappointed when my parents made a decision on my behalf that didn't quite align with my plans—or worse, was the complete opposite of what I wanted!

"It's not fair!" I'd cry. It didn't feel fair, but in several instances, I also distinctly remember feeling relieved that the decision had been taken out of my hands. My parents exercised wisdom when making decisions that were best for me instead of simply allowing me to have my way.

Now that I am a parent myself, I respect the boundaries they set for me. From time to time, my parents still lend their thoughts and advice when I have a difficult choice to make. Their guidance holds weight because I value the wisdom they've shown me my entire life. That doesn't mean they didn't let me experience life lessons that I needed to learn—and some were definitely more painful than others. However, the combination of the wisdom they modeled for me combined with my own life experiences taught me the value of making wise choices—and more importantly, seeking God's wisdom in any decision-making process.

It seems like a grown-up concept, but it's really not. Our kids have the opportunity to utilize wisdom every day— from small choices like eating their fruits and veggies instead of a cookie to bigger decisions such as not participating when a group of friends picks on another student. As a mom, I'm so thankful to share in these experiences with my daughters—whether or not they make wise choices.

I'm still thankful even when my daughters echo my own words of wisdom back at me when I least expect them. If it hasn't happened to you, just wait. It's a great reminder that we're all girls of grace in training!

CHAPTER 4

girl of grace characteristic:

HUMILITY

Who is the greatest?

When you work really hard to achieve a goal, you likely feel proud when you accomplish it. How we behave when we receive recognition or honor reflects our humility—or humbleness. Humility is not to be confused with humiliation. Stumbling in the hallway at school with an armload of books can definitely result in humiliation. However, humility is the feeling that even though you may be recognized for something wonderful and great,

> ### DID YOU KNOW?
>
> Did you know the word **humility** is actually derived from the Latin word **humilis**, which means low, humble, from the earth? A humble person is generally thought to be down-to-earth and modest.

you don't see yourself as really any different from anyone else. It's all about keeping yourself in the proper perspective.

What about the unique abilities and God-given gifts that make you who you are? There are no two people alike, and God did that intentionally! It's important to recognize that each and every one of us has special talents and gifts and that these special talents come from God. We are going to explore this concept more as we discuss this week's girls of grace characteristic: humility. Jesus's earthly mother, Mary, and a little servant girl named Rhoda are the focus of these explorations as we dig a little deeper into what it means to have humility.

Let's take a peek at Mary first. Scholars think Mary was about thirteen years old when she was approached by the angel Gabriel with news that she had been chosen to give birth to the Son of God. Do you remember how she reacted?

> *The angel went to her and said, "Greetings, you who are highly favored! The Lord is with you." Mary was greatly troubled at his words and wondered what kind of greeting this might be. But the angel said to her, "Do not be afraid, Mary; you have found favor with God."*
>
> Luke 1:28–30

The Bible tells us that Mary was concerned when she heard that she was highly favored. Here she thought of herself as a regular young Jewish girl from Galilee. Mary didn't think of herself as special and different, and she was confused when the angel Gabriel said she was highly favored. This is the picture of humility.

Mary didn't understand why God called her to this honor and journey, and she didn't need to understand. Mary accepted her path with simple faith and humility. She accepted that God recognized her as the uniquely gifted person he created, and Mary understood her gifting came from God.

Luke 1:48 tells us, "For he took notice of his lowly servant girl, and from now on all generations will call me blessed" (NLT). These words taken from Mary's song reflect her awe and gratitude and, ultimately, her worship of God for the gifts he bestowed upon her.

Scripture never tells us that Mary was full of pride at being chosen to bear the Son of God. She didn't brag to her friends or make boasts about her place in God's plan. Why?

Have you ever received an honor or been selected for a role that you didn't feel you deserved? You may not think you deserved the accolades you received, but others clearly recognized your hard work and talent. What you felt was humility!

Think about this. Imagine you and your friend are playing on a softball team. This isn't just any game. It's the play-off tournament! Whichever team wins this game will be crowned the season champion, and your team has worked so hard to be here! It's a good day for you, and you score three runs for your team. Your good friend scores the same. Another team member hits a home run in the last inning and helps your team win the game by one point.

After the game, your team naturally wants to celebrate! It's been an amazing season, and your teammates have played with all their hearts to win the championship. At school on Monday, your teammate who scored the last run of the game is bragging about how she single-handedly won the championship on the team's behalf. When asked about the six points you and your friend scored, you gently reply that winning the championship took all of your team members. No one team member accomplished it by herself.

Who do you think is more admired by their classmates: the team member who took all the credit for a great accomplishment or a team member who played well but recognized the hard work of everyone else around her? What you displayed by turning the limelight away from yourself was humility.

 girl of grace HEarT CHECK

- **Read Luke 1:46–55.** What does Mary's song of praise say God has done for her? Does she recognize her important place in God's plan, or does she give the glory to God?

- Do you think about God when you uncover a new talent you didn't realize you have or when your unique ability or gifting results in an award or praise? How do you respond?

♥ Philippians 2:3 says, "Do nothing out of selfish ambition or vain conceit. Rather, in humility value others above yourselves, not looking to your own interests but each of you to the interests of the others." Talk with your mom about what this means to you and how you can put others above yourself.

an activity for mom and me: scruB-a-DUB!

Read John 13:1–17. In this passage, Jesus is washing the feet of his disciples. Now read Luke 7:36–50. This time, a sinful woman is washing Jesus's feet. Now, it's your turn. Take a few minutes to gather the supplies you'll need:
   ♥ Basin (or bowl big enough for your feet)
   ♥ Water
   ♥ Soap
   ♥ Two clean towels

Take turns with your mom as you wash each other's feet. Use one towel to wipe away the dirt and one towel to dry the clean feet. Now, since we're girls, we can absolutely bring out the nail polish and paint those adorable tootsies after we've washed each other's feet. However, talk about why washing someone's feet is an act of humility. Why do you think Jesus used this particular activity with his disciples? Why was it so meaningful for the sinful woman to wash Jesus's feet?

No Task Too great or Small

The New Testament paints a picture of what it was like for early Christians who began building churches. These were the days after Jesus's resurrection when Christians met in secret because it was dangerous to meet in public places or in large groups. Herod Agrippa I, the Roman king, had ordered the persecution of Christians. As a result, members of the early church often met in homes and had to be careful about answering the door when other church members were present.

Rhoda was a young servant girl in one such home—the home of Mary, mother of the disciple, John Mark. Rhoda's story isn't long and is only mentioned in Acts 12:13–16.

> *Peter knocked at the outer entrance. A servant named Rhoda came to answer the door.*
>
> *She recognized Peter's voice. She was so excited that she ran back without opening the door. "Peter is at the door!" she exclaimed.*
>
> *"You're out of your mind," they said to her. But she kept telling them it was true.*
>
> *So they said, "It must be his angel."*
>
> *Peter kept on knocking. When they opened the door and saw him, they were amazed.*
>
> Acts 12:13–16 (NIRV)

A few things stand out about this amazing girl of grace, Rhoda. First, she was a servant. Her tasks were probably considered inconsequential or unimportant by those around her. Secondly, she was a girl. Rhoda was probably around twelve years old, so she would not have held a position of great authority or respect. However, this young girl had a passion for God and a persistence to be heard.

On this particular night, there was a church meeting in Mary's home, where Rhoda served. She went to answer a knock at the door and heard Peter's voice. In her excitement, she ran to the group meeting inside to say, "Peter's here! Peter's here! I heard his voice. He's here!"

The reason no one believed her was that Peter had been arrested and was supposed to be sitting in jail. The Roman king had Peter arrested for proclaiming his faith and had ordered guards around Peter night and day. Mary, Mark, and the other church members had been praying for Peter's release. They didn't know angels had interceded for Peter, and now he was free. They thought Rhoda was hearing Peter's spirit. Rhoda insisted until finally others followed her out to the gate, where there, indeed, was Peter!

What I love about Rhoda is her unbridled enthusiasm to welcome Peter. When she heard his voice, she was excited! She wasn't the least bit worried about Roman soldiers crashing the party. Rhoda ran to the crowd of believers gathered inside Mary's home to share her excitement that Peter was free and at their door. Even when the others didn't believe her and told her she was loony tunes, she insisted Peter was there.

Rhoda sets a brilliant example of humility for other girls of grace. She was a servant. She was a young girl who essentially had no voice, but God used little Rhoda! She is proof that God doesn't see us the way we see ourselves. She also models for us that sometimes God asks us to serve in tasks where we don't receive honor and glory from those around us, and that's okay. Rhoda answered a door. That may not seem like a very important job, but she recognized immediately that God had answered their prayers to free Peter.

Even though you may sometimes feel your role in God's plan is not important, I can assure you that you are very important to God's kingdom. God does occasionally ask us to serve him in a big way, but we can serve him in small ways every day. Can you think of a few ways God is using you?

WHO NEEDS PRIDE?

One of our family's favorite Wii games is from a popular dancing series. Not only is it great exercise, but it is also loads of fun! I grew up dancing and love to cut a rug with my baby girls. However, their sweet father has absolutely no rhythm (which he readily admits).

Although my husband is rhythmically challenged, he is always eager to engage in a "Just Dance" dance-off! Well, maybe "eager" is too strong a word. The point is that he sets aside his pride and fear of looking foolish to build wonderful memories with his daughters. There's always plenty of laughing when the Wii remotes are in hand!

And dancing may not be my husband's greatest strength, but he is tough to beat with a hula hoop!

♥ How is the way that Rhoda served God like or different from the way you serve him? What about you, Mom?

♥ Look up the definition of "persecution." Early Christians were openly mocked and bullied for their beliefs. Rhoda was delighted when she realized God had answered the prayer to free Peter and didn't seem worried that the church members gathered in Mary's home were in danger. Do you feel like you can share your faith openly with your friends and at school? Talk with your mom about why or why not.

♥ Brainstorm with your mom a way you two can serve God "behind the scenes" this week. After you've put your plan into action, talk about how it made you feel to serve God anonymously.

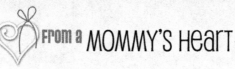

From a MOMMY'S HEART

As mothers, we are given countless opportunities to serve God behind the scenes. Raising strong daughters who aren't afraid to speak their minds is important, but it's just as vital to teach our baby girls the value of humility. I am the first to admit that this mommy is still a girl of grace in training. No matter how many wonderful chats I think my daughters and I have, nothing speaks louder to them than my actions.

I've been an active member of the Junior League since I was in my midtwenties. Through the years, my girls have often seen me preparing for meetings and organizing one event or another. These sweet girls have attended numerous League functions and been to the League office more times than I can count—and soaked up every detail. I remember one day a few years ago coming across my girls and their cousins in our dining room. They had collected clipboards and pens and had organized their chairs in a semicircle. They looked so serious and seemed to be in deep discussion. When I asked them what they were doing, they quickly replied, "We're having a Junior League meeting."

At the time, I was tickled. However, when I thought about the impact of my actions on the two girls that God has placed in my care, their "meeting" weighed more heavily on me. It made me conscious of the perception my girls were taking away from the way I was serving others. This encounter opened the door for conversations about how we can serve others, and about how serving can look different to every individual. Regardless of which community organization you may support or how you choose to volunteer your time, we have the opportunity to teach our daughters the importance of serving God and our community in quiet ways. It's more than having a servant's heart, which we'll talk about in Chapter Six.

I didn't begin volunteering to earn accolades or get a pat on the back. I first volunteered at the Special Olympics when I was in high school. My job was to hug participants as they came across the finish line. Everyone got a hug, and it was awesome! Those moments were not about who finished first; they were about making every individual feel valued. That's why I continue to volunteer and why I want to teach my girls that you can serve God with humility when you serve others in need. You don't do it for the credit. You don't donate money for the tax write-off. We serve because God calls us to love one another.

girl of grace characteristic:

courage

courage is acting in spite of fear!

Have you ever felt afraid? What does being afraid feel like to you? Does your heart start to beat faster? Do your palms begin to sweat?

What makes you feel scared? Maybe you have felt fear before a dance recital, a performance, or a big game. Perhaps you have been afraid of how the first day of school would go or of trying a new experience for the first time. Or it could be that taking medicine when you are sick makes your belly do crazy flip-flops. Growing up, I was afraid of the dark for years—truly. I can remember preparing a pallet in my doorway each evening so that I would be that much closer to my parents' bedroom should I need their help in the middle of the night. And yes! I absolutely tested how long it would take me to run down that hall on more than one occasion.

The point is that we have all felt afraid at one time or another during our lives. Being scared is a very normal, very common feeling. Has your fear ever kept you from facing what you dreaded? Did you skip that big game or performance or decide to stay home from school? Did you refuse to take that foul-tasting medicine that your body needed to get well? No! Chances are that you acted in spite of the fear you were feeling. What you showed in the face of your fear was courage!

Courage—this is the girls of grace characteristic that we are going to discuss in this chapter. Esther and Rahab share the spotlight this week as our role models from the Bible and demonstrate for us what it means to act courageously even when you may feel afraid.

Esther lived in a time when a Persian king named Xerxes ruled over the Israelites. Since both of Esther's parents were dead, she was raised by her loving uncle Mordecai who was a Jewish official in King Xerxes's royal court. Esther was taken against her will from her uncle Mordecai's home at a fairly young age to live in the palace alongside other pretty girls from the city. Her beauty was renowned, and eventually King Xerxes named Esther queen.

King Xerxes was a pagan and did not believe in God. Esther was a Jewish girl who was raised by her uncle to love and honor God. Uncle Mordecai found favor with the king when he overheard a plot of traitors who planned to kill King Xerxes. However, Haman—King Xerxes's most powerful official—did not like Mordecai because he refused to bow to Haman. Mordecai told Haman that he would only bow before God.

Well, you can imagine how well that news was received. Haman was pretty mad! In fact, he was so mad that he convinced King Xerxes to kill all the Jews. Mordecai was afraid and sent word to his niece, Queen Esther, to plead with the king for their lives. She knew Haman's intentions were evil and agreed to help. She sent word back to her uncle that he and the other Jews should fast and pray for three days.

It was the custom of those days that no one ever approached the king unless he summoned them first. To approach the king or request an audience could mean certain death! Queen Esther knew that asking to see her king was a dangerous mission, and she was surely afraid of how he might respond.

> Then Esther told Hathach to go back and relay this message to Mordecai: "All the king's officials and even the people in the provinces know that anyone who appears before the king in his inner court without being invited is doomed to die unless the king holds out his gold scepter. And the king has not called for me to come to him for thirty days." So Hathach gave Esther's message to Mordecai.
>
> Mordecai sent this reply to Esther: "Don't think for a moment that because you're in the palace you will escape when all other Jews are killed. If you keep quiet at a time like this, deliverance and relief for the Jews will arise from some other place, but you and your relatives will die. Who knows if perhaps you were made queen for just such a time as this?"
>
> Then Esther sent this reply to Mordecai: "Go and gather together all the Jews of Susa and fast for me. Do not eat or drink for three days, night or day. My maids and I will do the same. And then, though it is against the law, I will go in to see the king. If I must die, I must die."
>
> Esther 4:10–16 (NLT)

King Xerxes accepted Esther's request and she was ultimately able to tell him about Haman's evil plans. She also reminded the king that one of the men to be killed was the same man who had saved the king's life! When King Xerxes checked his book of records, he found Esther was right. Haman's plan backfired; the king executed him instead of Mordecai and the other Jews.

Think of what would have happened if God had not given Esther the courage to stand before her king. Esther must have been frightened, but she acted in spite of her fear in order to save the lives of thousands of Jews.

We have opportunities to exercise courage every day. Occasionally, God may use each of us in a big way like he did with Esther. However, just because we aren't saving a nation on this particular day doesn't mean we have to miss an opportunity to honor God through other courageous actions. What acts of bravery have you encountered today?

Have your friends ever picked on another classmate, and you knew what they were doing was wrong? Do you have the courage to be kind to the person your friends are ridiculing even if it means they will no longer want to be friends with you?

Read Matthew 25:35–40 in the sidebar. Jesus calls us to serve those who are less fortunate. Serving people who are different from you takes courage! Have you ever participated in a mission trip or mission project where

SERVING GOD BY SERVING OTHERS

"Then the King will say to those on his right, 'Come, you who are blessed by my Father; take your inheritance, the kingdom prepared for you since the creation of the world. For I was hungry and you gave me something to eat, I was thirsty and you gave me something to drink, I was a stranger and you invited me in, I needed clothes and you clothed me, I was sick and you looked after me, I was in prison and you came to visit me.'

"Then the righteous will answer him, 'Lord, when did we see you hungry and feed you, or thirsty and give you something to drink? When did we see you a stranger and invite you in, or needing clothes and clothe you? When did we see you sick or in prison and go to visit you?'

"The King will reply, 'Truly I tell you, whatever you did for one of the least of these brothers and sisters of mine, you did for me."

—Matthew 25:34–40

you had the opportunity to serve the sick, the poor, the elderly, or someone else who was in need of prayer and support?

Or perhaps you feel God asking you to approach someone you may not know and offer words of encouragement. Maybe God is asking you to try something that has never been done before and you are afraid of failing. Both of these callings—as well as many other actions God calls us to do—take courage!

I'm sure you can think of other examples of courage that you encounter every single day. Perhaps there are others around you who inspire you through their own acts of bravery. Isn't it cool to think that God is very possibly using you in that same way?

an activity for mom and me: THE Courage TO BE DIFFERENT

When my girls were younger, we loved playing dress up together. They would take turns trying on all of my shoes and putting on makeup. One particular day, my girls had really given me the star treatment. Makeup was strewn across my bathroom. They had also styled my hair—and used every bow they could reach with their precious little fingers. They worked so hard to make me look fabulous!

Well, as mommies tend to do, I got distracted after playtime and moved on to other things. Late in the day, I realized that I'd forgotten to pick up our dry cleaning. My husband was leaving town and needed his clothes, so I loaded the girls into the car quickly and dashed to the cleaner before closing time. Well, closing time at the cleaner's is like a Friday night football game . . . it's really busy. No matter! I waited in line with my girls, listening to their chatter.

I noticed that I was getting some strange looks, but I chalked it up to me wrangling my active sweet peas in such a small space. When I got to the counter, the clerk just stared at me. I smiled politely and gave her my last name. She stood there for a moment longer and then rushed off to grab our dry cleaning. Minutes later, more eyes were peering from the back of the cleaners. I remember thinking it was the strangest behavior I'd ever encountered, but I still wasn't too worried.

girl of grace HEART CHECK

♥ **Read Esther 7:1–10.** Talk with your mom about what was at stake for Queen Esther as she pleaded for the lives of her people. Have you ever stood up for someone you knew was being wronged? Has anyone shown courage by standing up for you? How did you feel afterward?

The clerk came back with our clothes and continued to stare as I thanked her and ushered my girls back to the car. When we were in the car, I commented on the clerk's strange behavior in the store. My oldest darling then replied, "Maybe she thought your hair was so beautiful!"

Then it hit me. I closed my eyes and lifted my face toward the rearview mirror. Slowly, I opened my eyes and immediately wanted to sink into a hole. Staring back at me was the mommy who had let her babies put blue eye shadow, red blush, and lipstick on her face. Of course, complimenting that lovely complexion was a sophisticated hairstyle with about thirty bows of various shapes and colors. Mortified doesn't begin to cover it.

After the humiliation passed, my girls talked for weeks about how beautiful their mommy looked on the day she let them fix her hair and makeup. I thought, "It's okay to be different!"

Okay, girls! It's your turn! This activity is all about the courage to be different. You're going to play dress up. You can be as silly or sophisticated as you like! The goal is to dress together and pick a public place for lunch, dinner, or some fun errand.

Society can pressure us that as girls and ladies, we need to conform to a certain image. You and your mom are going to have fun showing that it's okay to have the courage to be different. Embrace the individuality that God gave you, and take time to celebrate the girl of grace he has made in you.

♥ Sure, it takes courage to sing in front of a crowd or walk home alone at night. However, we sometimes have to dig deep within our spirits for courage to face scary situations. Have you ever had to defend your faith or your family?

♥ Can you think of a time when you knew you should speak from your heart, but you couldn't find your voice to say anything? How did you handle this situation? God doesn't waste any experience, so there is most likely something you learned from your circumstances. Take turns sharing thoughts with your mom.

♥ Sometimes, others perceive Christians as being judgmental instead of kind. Why does it take courage to show others that being a Christian means loving one another?

courage rewarded

Our next girl of grace is Rahab, a woman who didn't have the best reputation in Jericho. She was probably not a traveler's first choice of hostess. However, when Joshua's spies came into the city before it fell, Rahab sheltered them. Now, let's just take a minute and think about this.

Imagine two spies come to your front door. Your country is in danger of war, and everyone is terrified of what might happen. When these guys arrive on your doorstep, you know they are spies and that helping them could mean death for your entire family. You let them into your house anyway and agree to protect them until they can escape the city at nightfall.

When the police come to your door, your heart is beating so hard that it just might pop right out of your chest. Those two spies are hiding in your closet! You tell the policemen at your door that you did see those rascally spies earlier in the day, but they are long gone. Then you suggest the police look on the other side of town, since you think that is where the men were trying to escape to.

It feels dramatic, but it was a big deal for Rahab. She was committing treason, but she also knew her city was about to fall into the hands of Joshua's army. She courageously protected Joshua's spies knowing they could be caught and put to death at any time.

When the city fell, Rahab and her family were spared because of the courage she showed. Besides Rahab and her family, no one in the city of Jericho was left alive—not one person! Even the animals and livestock were killed. Rahab and her family's survival was significant!

When the trumpets sounded, the army shouted, and at the sound of the trumpet, when the men gave a loud shout, the wall collapsed; so everyone charged straight in, and they took the city. They devoted the city to the LORD and destroyed with the sword every living thing in it—men and women, young and old, cattle, sheep and donkeys.

Joshua said to the two men who had spied out the land, "Go into the prostitute's house and bring her out and all who belong to her, in accordance with your oath to her." So the young men who had done the spying went in and brought out Rahab, her father and mother, her brothers and sisters and all who belonged to her. They brought out her entire family and put them in a place outside the camp of Israel.

Then they burned the whole city and everything in it, but they put the silver and gold and the articles of bronze and iron into the treasury of the LORD's house. But Joshua spared Rahab the prostitute, with her family and all who belonged to her, because she hid the men Joshua had sent as spies to Jericho—and she lives among the Israelites to this day.

Joshua 6:20–25

While it's not likely you will have foreign spies appear at your door anytime soon, it is likely that you are engaging in acts of bravery every single day—and possibly without even realizing it! While you may find it quite comfortable to present a project in front of your class, Sally Sue may be utterly terrified at the thought of speaking in front of her classmates. Martha may love dogs of all shapes and sizes, but being near a furry critter may make your teeth chatter with fear.

Esther and Rahab help us realize that while we may not understand their exact situation and feelings, we can appreciate the courage they showed in the face of their fears. Like all our girls of grace characteristics, courage comes from God. Courage comes from the belief that he is with us and will see us through whatever we feel is scary or potentially harmful. When you exercise courage and give God the glory, God is able to use you to reach others who may not know him the way you do. He is very likely using your acts of courage without you even knowing it! So think about that the next time you're facing one of your fears.

♥ Have you ever been influenced by someone else's act of courage? What was it? Take turns sharing stories with your mom.

♥ Who is the most courageous person you know? Why do you think that person is courageous? What about the least courageous person you know? Pray for this person by name this week and ask God to equip them with courage and whatever else they need to face their circumstances.

♥ What is your biggest fear? Have you ever faced it? Ask Mom to share her biggest fear, too. Pray for one another this week, and ask God for the courage to help you conquer the things that make you afraid.

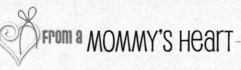

FROM a MOMMY'S HeaRT

One of the toughest life lessons is developing the courage to stand for what you believe. We teach our little ones as babies to have courage to crawl and then to walk. We teach them to be brave as we leave them for the first time in childcare and then remind ourselves to have the courage to leave them there. Life skills like this are all part of normal growth and development.

Just as learning to walk, talk, and be independent are important life skills for our children to learn, so is the characteristic of courage. The experiences we have as children often mold or influence the adults we become. Some of us find our voices sooner than others, but some of us never find the courage to stand for what we believe.

Fifth grade was the first time I recall struggling with the courage (or lack thereof) to stand up to my friends. Girls are especially vulnerable to others' opinions, especially the people (small and tall) they hold in high regard. My girls and I often have conversations about why it is okay to have different perspectives from our friends—that having different perspectives and being able to let your friend know when you feel differently about a topic is a good thing. I tell my girls that their favorite color doesn't have to be blue because their best friend's favorite color is blue.

Having the courage to stand up in a situation when the popular opinion is stacked against you is tough, but sometimes it's more difficult to find courage to be honest and hold our friends accountable when their actions clash with the people God has called us to be. Developing courage like this takes time, prayer, and a loving example from Mom and Dad.

I've mentioned it before, but I am a girl of grace in training, too! These notes from a mommy's heart are just that. These are thoughts and concerns that I lay before God as my husband and I prayerfully guide our daughters through the crazy obstacle course of life. This world is broken, but these sweet girls of grace are not. We can teach them to pray and pray with them that God will instill the courage they need to navigate these sometimes dangerous waters.

girl of grace characteristic:

WITNESSING
THROUGH a servant's Heart

serving god by serving others

On one of our few cold Texas days last year, I decided to drive through Starbucks and get a cup of hot chocolate. Their salted caramel hot cocoa is my favorite! The line was long, and I was feeling a little grumpy from dealing with all the other Christmas shoppers who apparently were just as disgruntled as I felt. Anyway, I finally arrived at the window where I took my yummy beverage from the smiling Starbucks cashier. When I asked her to remind me how much I owed, she replied, "Nothing. The car in front of you paid for your drink."

She continued to smile as I'm sure my startled expression showed how confused I felt. She pointed to the car in front of me that had waited to see me pick up my drink. They waved and shouted, "Merry Christmas!"

I felt myself smile and returned the wave. Then, I turned to the lady at the window and told her I'd like to pay for the car behind me. She smiled and gave me their total. Like the car before me, I waited to see the customer's

---

a servant Calling

Then they began to argue among themselves about who would be the greatest among them. Jesus told them, "In this world the kings and great men lord it over their people, yet they are called 'friends of the people.' But among you it will be different. Those who are the greatest among you should take the lowest rank, and the leader should be like a servant. Who is more important, the one who sits at the table or the one who serves? The one who sits at the table, of course. But not here! For I am among you as one who serves."

—Luke 22:24–27 (NLT)

face when they arrived at the window to get their coffee only to be told it had already been purchased for them. I smiled, waved, and called out, "Merry Christmas!"

One act of service planted a seed for another. What happened to me that morning at Starbucks is what happens when we tend to others with a servant's heart. I was inspired by the kindness of the person in front of me in the drive-thru, and that inspiration led me to serve someone else in the same way. This is what we call witnessing through a servant's heart—our girl of grace topic for this week!

God calls us to love and care for one another. This week, we are going to investigate what happens when someone serves others for the sake of serving others and what impact their selflessness has on those they help. Dorcas and Phoebe, two women who served others quietly and often without recognition, hold the spotlight this week. You may not be as familiar with these two names as you are with Mary, Esther, or Ruth, but these ladies of the Bible play just as important a role as the more visible women we've talked about before them. Serving behind the scenes is important work for a girl of grace!

Dorcas knew what it meant to serve God by serving others. She was a widow who lived in the town of Joppa, one of the main seaports of Judea at the time (and the same port Jonah came to when he was running from God). Dorcas's story can be found in Acts 9:36–42.

In Joppa there was a disciple named Tabitha (in Greek her name is Dorcas); she was always doing good and helping the poor. About that time she became sick and died, and her body was washed and placed in an upstairs room. Lydda was near Joppa; so when the disciples heard that Peter was in Lydda, they sent two men to him and urged him, "Please come at once!"

Peter went with them, and when he arrived he was taken upstairs to the room. All the widows stood around him, crying and showing him the robes and other clothing that Dorcas had made while she was still with them.

Peter sent them all out of the room; then he got down on his knees and prayed. Turning toward the dead woman, he said, "Tabitha, get up." She opened her eyes, and seeing Peter she sat up. He took her by the hand and helped her to her feet. Then he called for the believers, especially the widows, and presented her to them alive. This became known all over Joppa, and many people believed in the Lord.

Acts 9:36–42

Dorcas was known for serving the poor in her community, and she was dearly loved for her acts of service. Her special talent was making clothes for other people, which is what Dorcas's mourners showed to Peter when he arrived in Joppa to pray for her. There wasn't anything especially remarkable about Dorcas. She was a widow who quietly made clothes and gave them to those who couldn't afford to buy their own. She wasn't widely revered or known throughout the world, but Dorcas was loved and respected in her own town. She modeled servanthood in the early days of the Christian church when the concept of serving Jesus by serving others was still very new.

From what we know of Dorcas, she didn't preach publicly (which would have been very unusual for a female in her day). She was not filthy rich. She was an ordinary lady in a busy seaport town who used her talent of sewing to serve those less fortunate. And God used her servant's heart mightily!

The passage in Acts that shares Dorcas's story tells us the widows were beside themselves with grief at her death. They cried and cried as they showed Peter all the clothes Dorcas had made for others. Peter was moved by their love for Dorcas and the service she had done, and he prayed that God would restore her. Dorcas came back to life! The Bible tells us that many others became believers when news spread of the miracle God performed for her. He used Dorcas's servant heart to witness to others who didn't know him and strengthened the faith of others who did.

girl of grace HEART CHECK

♥ To witness means to testify or declare a truth publicly. After reading Dorcas's story, why do you think the people of her town held her in such high regard?

♥ **Read Matthew 25:34–40.** Dorcas is the only female named as a "disciple" in the Bible. We know disciples are followers of Jesus and strive to serve others as Jesus did. What kind of call to action is written in the passage above? Do you think Dorcas's life reflects an answer to this calling? Talk with your mom about how you can answer this call to action as a girl of grace today.

♥ Is there a ministry or organization that has a mission you connect with? What about Mom? Take time this week to investigate ways you can volunteer or help this service or group of people.

ready and willing

Do you know anyone who has never needed assistance? Can you think of one name? I can't! That is because we all need help at some point in our lives. I need help on a daily basis! Think of all the responsibilities we have each and every day. Everyone needs a helper from time to time, and the apostle Paul was no different! One of his helpers was a woman named Phoebe. She is only mentioned in two verses of the Bible, but those two verses tell us how important Phoebe's service was to the kingdom of God.

> *I commend to you our sister Phoebe, who is a servant of the church which is at Cenchrea; that you receive her in the Lord in a manner worthy of the saints, and that you help her in whatever matter she may have need of you; for she herself has also been a helper of many, and of myself as well.*

Romans 16:1–2 (NASB)

Paul's short, but meaningful, commendation of Phoebe tells us four things about this girl of grace. First, she was a sister of Christ and a member of the early church. Second, Paul says that she is a "servant of the church." This was an honored title, and some scholars believe this means she held the office of deaconess or some other appointed role. By the very definition of the word "servant," she was a person who aided or helped others in need. Third, Paul requests that Phoebe be received in "a manner worthy of the saints." Wow! Think of the importance Paul was placing on Phoebe's service! Last, Paul asks that Phoebe be given any assistance she needs, because she has been a "helper to many" and to Paul himself.

We have no idea how old Phoebe was, what she looked like, whether she was rich or poor—and it's okay that we don't know these details about her. They weren't important. What is important was her commitment to serving God, his church and her fellow Christian brothers and sisters. As a helper and a servant, Phoebe stood ready to help when and where she was needed.

Jesus is the heart of what we call a "servant leader." He led by example and showed others what it means to spread the gospel by simply being a helper. As we discussed previously, God does occasionally ask us to fill big, important roles that result in public praise for our work. However, God's girls of grace have opportunities to spread the gospel every day just as Jesus did—by simply being a helper to others.

What does this look like for you? Maybe this looks like loaning a pencil in class to someone who has been mean to you and doing so with a tender heart and a warm smile. Perhaps it looks like sitting with the student at lunch who always sits alone. It could look like a regular volunteer commitment at your church, a local nursing home, or some other community-service project. Like Phoebe, you can be a servant by standing ready and willing to help when and where you are needed.

an activity for mom and me: your call to service

This week is about tapping into your servant's heart to help others. Hundreds of thousands of nonprofit organizations across the country exist to serve less fortunate members of our communities. Take some time this week to investigate what volunteer opportunities are available in your area. Nonprofit organizations sometimes have age requirements, so be sure to ask about those if you would like to volunteer on-site with a specific group.

Here are a few ideas to get you started:

* Serving in the pantry at a food bank
* Preparing bags of nutritious food, soap, and first-aid supplies for the homeless
* Reading to sick children at your local hospital or children's clinic
* Cleaning out your closets and making a donation to your local Goodwill or Salvation Army
* Preparing cards and donating games to a local nursing home or assisted-living facility for the elderly

The purpose of this Mom and Me activity is to find a serving opportunity that is meaningful for you. Sadly, there are countless community members who are in need of some type of assistance. You may wonder what one girl of grace can do, but you will be surprised at the impact your service has on others. While we honor God often with our pennies, we can also honor God by serving others who are unable to help themselves.

♥ Brainstorm with your mom about what it means to you to be a servant. Now talk about what it means to be a leader. What do you think it means to be a servant leader?

♥ Matthew 23:11 says, "The greatest among you will be your servant." Talk with your mom about what this means. Is God asking you to be a slave to your baby brother? Is he asking you to become a housekeeper? How does this passage apply to you?

♥ What are some ways you can make a difference by serving others? Make a list (Mom, too!) and see if you can put three ideas into action this week.

From a MOMMY'S HEarT - - - - - - - - - - -

One of the most poignant stories I love from the Bible is the story of the widow's offering. I'll admit this isn't a passage that spoke to me until I became a wife and mommy. The story can be found in Mark 12:41–44 and Luke 21:1–4.

> *Jesus sat down near the collection box in the Temple and watched as the crowds dropped in their money. Many rich people put in large amounts. Then a poor widow came and dropped in two small coins.*
>
> *Jesus called his disciples to him and said, "I tell you the truth, this poor widow has given more than all the others who are making contributions. For they gave a tiny part of their surplus, but she, poor as she is, has given everything she had to live on."*
>
> Mark 12:41–44 (NLT)

When I was a little girl, I thought a dollar was a lot of money. As adults, we realize how different our big-people perceptions are from our little selves. I can remember dropping money into the offering plate and feeling like I had made such a difference. I'm not sure when my perspective changed, but at some point I began to wonder how my little pennies could help when there always seemed to be such a great need.

Fast forward to being a wife and a mommy. We've had good years and years that were not so great. My husband lost his job during both of my pregnancies in the seventh month. We learned to live very leanly, and sometimes we wondered how in the world we could tithe when we could barely make our monthly bills. It was during these times that I realized just how important it was to give of my time and treasures. Even when we couldn't afford to give as much as we would have liked, my husband and I gave. We volunteered.

Our girls have taken notice. I truly believe God doesn't waste any experience—good or bad. What felt like really tough years have imprinted on my girls' hearts the importance of serving others. Those were the years when we volunteered more of our time because we couldn't afford to write that big check.

The story of the widow's offering continues to deeply touch me, because God wants us to serve from the heart. Jesus was sitting and watching rich folks drop all kinds of wonderful offerings into the box, but it was the widow's two coins that meant the most. It was all she had to give, and she gave with love and a full heart. What a witness to serving!

As parents, we act as those servant witnesses for our own kiddos. Sure, they learn and absorb from school and others around them—all the more reason for the witnessing they get at home to be just as visible and just as impactful. My girls find joy in serving others, as most children do. Think of the all the lemonade stands you've visited! My prayer as a mommy is that my girls maintain their excitement and exuberance of being such tender helpers as they continue to grow in this world that is in desperate need of servant leaders.

CHAPTER 7

Girl of Grace Characteristic:

Being a
GODLY Leader

Putting it all Together

Through Chapter Six, we've talked about several girl of grace characteristics:

- In Chapter One, Eve, Naomi, and Ruth modeled for us what it means to show **love**.
- Sarah, Mary, and Elizabeth held the spotlight in Chapter Two as we discussed what it means to have **faith**.
- Deborah, Miriam, and Abigail beautifully demonstrated through their stories in Chapter Three how to use God's gift of **wisdom**.
- In Chapter Four, Mary and a little servant girl named Rhoda showed us how to exercise **humility**.
- We explored the **courage** of Esther and Rahab in Chapter Five.
- And most recently, in Chapter Six we studied how Dorcas and Phoebe's powerful ministries were reflected in the way these two ladies **witnessed** to others **through their servant hearts**.

So what happens when you combine all of these girl grace characteristics? You get a godly leader! All the ladies we've discussed up to this point reflect godly leadership, but we are going to take a closer look at two women in particular as we delve into what the characteristic "godly leadership" really means. The first girl of grace is Lydia, and her story can be found in Acts 16:6–15.

> *Next Paul and Silas traveled through the area of Phrygia and Galatia, because the Holy Spirit had prevented them from preaching the word in the province of Asia at that time. Then coming to the borders of Mysia, they headed north for the province of Bithynia, but again the Spirit of Jesus did not allow them to go there. So instead, they went on through Mysia to the seaport of Troas.*

That night Paul had a vision: A man from Macedonia in northern Greece was standing there, pleading with him, "Come over to Macedonia and help us!" So we decided to leave for Macedonia at once, having concluded that God was calling us to preach the Good News there.

We boarded a boat at Troas and sailed straight across to the island of Samothrace, and the next day we landed at Neapolis. From there we reached Philippi, a major city of that district of Macedonia and a Roman colony. And we stayed there several days.

On the Sabbath we went a little way outside the city to a riverbank, where we thought people would be meeting for prayer, and we sat down to speak with some women who had gathered there. One of them was Lydia from Thyatira, a merchant of expensive purple cloth, who worshiped God. As she listened to us, the Lord opened her heart, and she accepted what Paul was saying. She and her household were baptized, and she asked us to be her guests. "If you agree that I am a true believer in the Lord," she said, "come and stay at my home." And she urged us until we agreed.

Acts 16:6–15 (NLT)

Even though Lydia is technically only mentioned in six verses (Acts 16:11–15; 40) of the Bible, we are able to tell a lot about this girl of grace. At the time Lydia lived, the old law said a town or city needed ten reliable Jewish men in order to have a synagogue. Phillipi did not have enough Jewish support at the time, which is why Lydia and the other women were worshipping on the riverbank outside the city—where Paul and Silas found them.

It's important to note that Lydia is the only name mentioned, while Paul's account makes it clear there were other women present. We know from what Paul shared that Lydia was a successful businesswoman, because he said she was "a merchant of purple cloth." Purple dye was an expensive luxury item in those days, and it is very likely that Lydia was a wealthy business owner. We know she ran a household with servants, who followed her example of accepting Jesus into her heart and being baptized in the Christian faith.

Here was a lady who was successful, wealthy, and probably wanted for little. Yet, she was hungry to learn more about the loving God who sent his only son to die for the sins of humankind. For all her earthly wealth, Lydia realized she had nothing without God. She not only became a woman of faith, her home became the primary meeting place for Paul's church ministry in Philippi.

What makes Lydia a godly leader? She had both presence and commitment. Lydia was present on the riverbank and listened with an open heart. When Paul and the other missionaries sat with the women on the riverbank, she recognized the calling God was placing on her heart and answered. Lydia expressed immediate love for the God who created her and showed her faith by accepting him into her heart. She didn't just show up for prayer meetings, Lydia jumped into faith with everything she had.

Lydia opened her home to Paul, Silas, and other Christians. The early days of the church were dangerous, yet Lydia showed courage as she welcomed other believers into her home time and time again. Even though she was a wealthy merchant, Lydia's humility enabled her to worship beside other believers who may not have held her same social status.

This girl of grace heard God's call, answered that calling and served the church where, when, and how she was needed. Lydia held nothing back (spiritually or materially), and she led by example. She could have ordered her servants and household to obey her without question, but Lydia guided her household by stepping out in faith first. She had courage to walk a path less traveled, and those who lived with and around her followed Lydia's lead.

God created each and every one of his girls of grace for a unique and meaningful purpose. Whether you are serving visibly or less noticeably, we all have the opportunity to play the part of Godly leaders.

Think of every time you have made a decision to honor God through your life choices. You may not be aware, but in all of those instances, someone is taking notice. You are leading someone closer to God simply by exercising your girls of grace traits. That is what being a godly leader means.

It's not about accepting that role on student council—although God can absolutely work through you in leadership positions like this. Remember, God calls people into all kinds of leadership opportunities— church leadership, peer leadership (which may be as simple as taking more responsibility in your class), and social leadership (which may look like organizing a group of friends to volunteer for a community service project). You don't have to be a grown-up to lead in these ways. But leadership is more than the roles we serve in; it is the way we behave. It's not about placing yourself above others. It's not about delegating or telling others what they should be doing. It's living your faith out loud. Godly leaders are those who serve for the sake of God, not for their own sake. Have you answered God's calling for your life? Are you living your faith aloud?

an activity for mom and me: recognizing GODLY Leaders

In the questions to the right, you and your mom identified someone (or more than one person) who you think exhibits godly leadership. This is likely someone you admire and respect. Godly leaders are often on the spiritual front lines of service and are not typically serving others to benefit themselves. That being the case, these godly leaders likely aren't asking others to share how wonderful they are. Sometimes, God uses girls of grace like us as cheerleaders for other godly leaders.

This week's "Mom and Me" activity is about honoring a godly leader who has impacted your faith walk. Decide between your mom and yourself how you would like to honor the person or people you identified.

Here are a few ideas to get you started:

♥ Drop a card in the mail.

♥ Deliver home-baked cookies.

♥ Arrange to volunteer with their ministry or help them in some way (If this is a teacher, you could offer to make copies or clean the boards during recess!).

♥ Take your godly leader to lunch.

The purpose of this week's activity is taking time to let this individual know they are making a difference to you. Tell them why you think they are a godly leader and how you are praying for them. Your love and affirmation may be just what they need to hear when they need to hear it.

♥ Who comes to mind when you think of a godly leader you know personally? What makes this person (or persons) a godly leader in your eyes? Compare your thoughts with your mom's. How are your points of view different? How are they the same?

♥ Look back at the list of women we have discussed in our girls of grace Bible study. Which of these godly leaders do you relate to best? Why? Ask Mom to share who she connects with the most. Are they different or the same?

♥ What does it mean to lead by example? Is this something you do? Talk with your mom about why you think a leader who leads by example is more respected than a leader who simply tells others what they should do.

Doing the Unexpected

Anna, a prophetess mentioned in the New Testament, is our second girl of grace for this week's topic. Her story is reflected in only three verses found within the book of Luke.

> *Anna, a prophet, was also there in the Temple. She was the daughter of Phanuel from the tribe of Asher, and she was very old. Her husband died when they had been married only seven years. Then she lived as a widow to the age of eighty-four. She never left the Temple but stayed there day and night, worshiping God with fasting and prayer. She came along just as Simeon was talking with Mary and Joseph, and she began praising God. She talked about the child to everyone who had been waiting expectantly for God to rescue Jerusalem.*
>
> Luke 2:36–38 (NLT)

In just three verses, we can actually tell a lot about Anna. First, she was widowed at a young age. After only seven years of marriage, Anna's husband died. Cultural customs of her day would have dictated that Anna return to her family's home until she married again. But that's not what Anna did.

Anna went to the temple, where she remained until she was eighty-four years old! She dedicated her life to praying and communing with God. The fact that she was given the title of prophetess means that Anna was able to interpret God's plans that had yet to pass. Anna oozed godly leadership by her very public portrayal of faith, love, wisdom, and servantship. It must have taken great courage, as well, to go against the cultural norm of her day by saying she was moving to the temple instead of back home with her family.

That's not to say Anna didn't honor her parents. She felt God calling her to a specific service, and she answered. Can you imagine? Anna's circumstances may be unique to her life in biblical times, but you can relate to her choice. For a girl of grace today, that may look like turning down an opportunity to play sports so that you have time for a special ministry that God has placed on your heart. That may be what God is asking of you! However, think of a time when a choice you made went against a popular or expected decision—but making that choice as you did honored God and your commitment to serving as a girl of grace.

Being a godly leader means sometimes making tough choices that aren't popular or understood by those around you. Did that stop Anna from answering the call God placed in her heart? It sure didn't. Being a godly leader doesn't necessarily mean you're leading a group of people. You are influencing and impacting others by your decision to stay true to your girl of grace mission.

The passage where we learn about Anna also says she immediately recognized who the baby with Mary and Joseph was, and she was excited! She told everyone about Jesus and how he would save us. She dedicated her entire life to fasting, praying, and serving God.

Anna was a remarkable godly leader, and her testimony is a good reminder for us that it's okay to do the unexpected. Her presence in three little verses is a powerful reminder over two thousand years later that godly leaders have the ability to reach others just simply by living as the girls of grace God has called us to be.

You may be called toward missions, a specific ministry with the church, social work, nonprofit work, or the military. Or perhaps God is calling you to serve him in another way. You don't have to be in a church ministry to serve God with your whole heart. Perhaps you may go on to be a corporate executive, a doctor, a politician, a teacher, or a stay-at-home mommy—the possibilities are endless. Regardless of the calling God places before you, remember you always have an opportunity to serve in that role as a godly leader. Whether you realize it or not, someone will take notice of your honorable choices.

♥ Can you think of a choice you've made that wasn't popular with your friends or those around you, but you knew in your heart it was what God was asking of you? Mom? How did others respond to your choice? How did you respond to their reaction?

♥ Anna made the decision to serve God night and day. Her service to him was very visible in that she lived at the temple, fasted, and prayed—day after day, year after year—until she was eighty-four years old! God doesn't call us all to this lifestyle. What are other ways you can lead by example when serving God?

From a MOMMY'S HEaRT

This week as I prayed about how to approach this topic, I kept circling back to how our actions are always visible to others—whether we realize it or not. How many times have we heard that children are little sponges and soak up everything they see and hear?

This week's topic is about our daughters being mindful of how their actions have the ability to influence others. As parents, we have a responsibility to exhibit godly leadership for our own children. This concept isn't always executed perfectly. Goodness knows, I make frequent mistakes, but I have learned these are teachable moments as well.

When my oldest daughter was potty training, we would praise her every time she went to the bathroom on the big-girl potty. We would clap ecstatically and cheer, "Good girl! Way to go!"

One day during this potty training season, my husband forgot to lock the bathroom door. Our daughter, who was less than three years old, pushed open the door and caught her daddy unaware. She gasped with delight and yelled, "Oh, good girl, Daddy! Good girl!"

Yes, it was funny. And no, we haven't let my husband forget about it. Little eyes and ears capture details adults would normally glaze over. Moments like these are funny, but kiddos also watch when Mommy forgives a friend who hurt her feelings. Or maybe it was Mommy who had to say she was sorry for hurting someone else. They watch when Mommy and Daddy put their tithe check into the offering plate. They watch when Mommy or Daddy takes dinner to a sick friend.

Guiding my two girls through life thus far has shown me that someone is always watching my every move, and it doesn't frighten me as it once did. I trust God to equip my husband and me with what we need to help our daughters continue their development into fearless godly leaders, so they will be ready and willing when God calls them into action.

girl of grace characteristic:

accountability

admitting when you've made a BOO·BOO

Who has ever broken the rules? Wouldn't we love to answer this question by saying, "Not me!"? We have all been there, though. The reality is that every single one of us has been reprimanded at one time or another for making a wrong choice. No one likes to be scolded. However, rules are important and are generally put in place for a reason.

Adam and Eve were given the very first rule. Do you remember what it was? Read Genesis 2:16–17.

> And the LORD God commanded the man, "You are free to eat from any tree in the garden; but you must not eat from the tree of the knowledge of good and evil, for when you eat from it you will certainly die."
>
> Genesis 2:16–17

God instructed Adam and Eve not to eat from the tree of the knowledge of good and evil. Well, we know what happened. The serpent deceived Eve, and she was the first to eat the forbidden fruit. Like a good partner, Eve wanted to share, so she encouraged Adam to eat from the tree as well. They broke the only rule God gave them!

Was God disappointed? Of course he was. Did he forgive Adam and Eve? Yes! Did their behavior go unpunished? No. God held them accountable for their choice to break the rules. There were consequences to Eve's choice. This brings us to our last girls of grace characteristic—accountability. This trait is about being responsible for your own actions and choices. All of the girls of grace we've discussed exhibit this important characteristic, but we're taking a closer look at the examples provided for us by Eve and Miriam.

When Eve ate from the tree of knowledge of good and evil, she felt guilty! She knew she had disobeyed God. When God asked her if she ate from the tree, she was honest. Eve admitted her sin. Admitting when you have made a mistake is not always an easy thing to do. It takes courage, but being able to admit when you are wrong is an important girl of grace trait.

Your parents hold you accountable when you make questionable decisions at home. Maybe telling that little white lie that your homework was finished is harmless. What happens, though, when you don't have time to finish your homework later and then have to explain to your parents not only why you lied, but why you didn't get full credit for your school assignment? That's no fun!

Throughout our lives, we are held accountable by different people—our parents, teachers, friends, bosses, and the church (just to name a few). Ultimately, though, it is God who holds us responsible for our choices and actions. Just like your mom and dad, God may be disappointed by a choice you make. Our parents tell us when we make bad choices, because it's their job as parents to help us learn the difference between actions that honor God (and ourselves!) and actions that do the opposite. Your mom and dad never stop loving you just because you make a mistake—just like God! When they hold you accountable, it is done out of love.

 girl of grace Heart Check

- ♥ Think of a time when you were caught doing something your mom or dad specifically asked you not to do. How did they respond? How did you respond to their reaction? Did being held accountable help you make a different choice the next time you found yourself in that situation?

♥ Look up the definition of "accountable" in a dictionary. Write the definition below. Talk with your mom about how you feel when you make a mistake and others hold you accountable. Do you feel differently when it's a parent, a teacher, a sibling, or a friend? How about Mom? Ask her how she feels to be held accountable?

Don't Hold a Grudge!

Have you ever gotten into an argument with a friend and then made up? But afterward, your friend constantly reminded you of why you made her mad in the first place. That's not holding someone accountable. That's holding a grudge!

Part of being a girl of grace means having the love, courage, and wisdom to hold others accountable when God calls you to do so. This could be as simple as gently reminding a friend to wait his or her turn in line at the movie. Occasionally, we all need a subtle (and sometimes not so subtle) nudge to help make the choice we know is right.

You remember Miriam, Moses's sister. We talked about her wisdom in Chapter Three. Miriam wisely watched her baby brother as he floated down the Nile River toward the pharaoh's palace. When she saw the pharaoh's daughter pick up the basket with Moses, Miriam offered to fetch a nurse for the baby. She was able to fetch their mother to care for Moses!

We all remember this story well. It turns out that God wasn't done working through Miriam. Miriam became a marvelous worship leader. "The Song of Moses and Miriam" found in Exodus 15 is not the only mention of Miriam's gift of song. She is discussed in the book of Numbers, as well.

Moses was said to be the most humble man alive, and Miriam and her brother, Aaron, became jealous of their baby brother. They started to say ugly things about Moses's wife and that God spoke to them as he spoke to Moses. God was angry with them for their bad behavior, and he called all three siblings together. See Numbers 12:1–15.

While they were at Hazeroth, Miriam and Aaron criticized Moses because he had married a Cushite woman. They said, "Has the Lord spoken only through Moses? Hasn't he spoken through us, too?" But the LORD heard them. (Now Moses was very humble—more humble than any other person on earth.)

So immediately the LORD called to Moses, Aaron, and Miriam and said, "Go out to the Tabernacle, all three of you!" So the three of them went to the Tabernacle. Then the LORD descended in the pillar of cloud and stood at the entrance of the Tabernacle. "Aaron and Miriam!" he called, and they stepped forward. And the LORD said to them, "Now listen to what I say:

"If there were prophets among you, I, the LORD, would reveal myself in visions. I would speak to them in dreams. But not with my servant Moses. Of all my house, he is the one I trust. I speak to him face to face, clearly, and not in riddles! He sees the LORD as he is. So why were you not afraid to criticize my servant Moses?"

The LORD was very angry with them, and he departed. As the cloud moved from above the Tabernacle, there stood Miriam, her skin as white as snow from leprosy. When Aaron saw what had happened to her, he cried out to Moses, "Oh, my master! Please don't punish us for this sin we have so foolishly committed. Don't let her be like a stillborn baby, already decayed at birth."

So Moses cried out to the LORD, "O God, I beg you, please heal her!"

But the LORD said to Moses, "If her father had done nothing more than spit in her face, wouldn't she be defiled for seven days? So keep her outside the camp for seven days, and after that she may be accepted back."

So Miriam was kept outside the camp for seven days, and the people waited until she was brought back before they traveled again.

Numbers 12:1–15 (NLT)

Oh, man! No one likes getting in trouble. I used to dread being called before my mom or dad when my brothers and I had been fighting. I knew before they ever said a word that I was guilty and wanted to say I was sorry for my part in the argument. I still had to face the consequences of my actions, though. My parents would always say, "We forgive you, and we love you. But you made a choice. All choices have consequences." They were holding me accountable for my actions.

That is what God did for Miriam. Her jealousy and choice to say mean things about her brother's wife made God angry. As a result, Miriam was punished for her actions. She was sorry for her choices, and Moses forgave her. He pleaded with God to show her mercy and grace. And God did—

an activity for mom and me: WaTCH IT GroW!

Accountability is all about owning personal responsibility. One of the best ways to demonstrate this concept is by taking on more responsibilities. That doesn't necessarily mean more house chores! This week, you are going to plant something from seed and watch it grow! Here's what you'll need:

- two clay pots (or flower pots of your choice)
- potting soil (be careful to purchase the right type of potting mix if you choose to plant fruits or veggies)
- flower, vegetable, or fruit seeds
- two tongue depressors
- markers
- water

Set aside some time to decorate your flower pots (if you chose a type that you can mark). Work with your mom to plant your seeds, and write the type of plant you picked on the tongue depressor. Place your tongue depressor in the potting soil after you have planted your seeds. Write your names (and the date) on the bottoms of the pot.

It's now time to watch them grow! However, in order for your plants to grow, you each have to take care of the seeds in your pot. You are now accountable for the health of your baby plant! Some plants may take longer to grow than others, so be patient, and have fun!

right after Miriam had her turn in the timeout corner. God forgave Miriam and restored her health so that she could take her place with her family again.

The wonderful example Miriam sets for us in this story is that her bad choice didn't keep her from making tons of other positive ones. We don't remember Miriam for that one awful situation. She is remembered for her wisdom at such a young age, and she is remembered for the amazing worship leader she became.

When you are accountable, that means you are willing to accept responsibility for your actions. When you hold someone else accountable, you do so with love, grace, and forgiveness. Those are the examples set for us by God's original girls of grace. We can learn from their experiences! And as you continue to grow and make choices, others will learn from you.

May God bless you, girls of grace!

 ## girl of grace HEART CHECK

♥ Why do you think it is important for us to be held accountable for our choices and actions? Ask your mom what she thinks.

♥ Can you think of a time when God used someone else to remind you to make a positive decision? Sometimes, we don't even realize we're being held accountable!

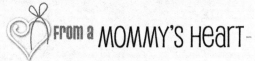

FROM a MOMMY'S HEART

A dear friend lost her earthly battle with cancer last Sunday—the same friend whose unshakeable faith I mentioned in Chapter Two. I first met her at a kindergarten social when our oldest kiddos started school. At that time, she had just completed her chemo and radiation treatments following her first breast cancer diagnosis. She was wearing a scarf on her bare head, and I remember being struck by her big, bright smile—which I would later come to know was nearly always on her face.

Thankfully, she was cancer free for more than three years. When our youngest children entered kindergarten, again in the same class, she learned that fall the cancer had returned. The next year would be a vicious battle to defeat the cancer cells that had invaded her body. Her positive voice and email updates never quite matched the news she was sharing.

She briefly went into remission after treatment for her second breast cancer diagnosis. Then, last April, I received an email from her late one night. It was a request for prayers as preliminary scans showed the cancer had returned and spread to the bone. I remember falling apart and being so angry. Sleep eluded me for a couple of nights as I prayed, pleaded, and ranted with God.

I ran into her after drop-off that week, and I remember walking over to her car. I gave her a big hug and told her I was really ticked off with God. My friend, who was battling stage 4 cancer, hugged me back and said, "That's okay. God can take it." She then went on to comfort me and reassure me about God's plan for our lives. Yes, she prayed for healing. Yes, she wanted to watch her boys grow up, graduate from college, get married. Yes, she wanted to grow old with her soul mate and best friend. Yet, she was okay with God's plan—whatever it was.

Last Sunday, her five-year battle with cancer finally ended. God did heal her, just not the way we asked for. You may be wondering what my friend's story has to do with the topic of accountability. At her funeral service, her husband stood before weeping family and friends. He shared that my friend's only request was that he tell everyone she wanted to spend eternity with them. She was adamant that he share with everyone at her service how to do just that.

As I sat and listened to her family and other friends share their experiences about my friend, one detail of my friend's life was glaringly evident. My friend lived her life mindful that she was accountable to God. When her boys (and her friends) struggled with the acceptance of her illness, she gently and firmly reminded them (and us) that we live in a broken world. God calls us to have faith. God calls us to live in faith.

Even after she departed, my friend was holding the rest of us accountable.

a JOINT BIBLE STUDY
FOr TWEEN GIRLS aND THEIr MOMS

Facilitator's guide

explaining the Format of This study

This study is unique in that it is not broken down by daily reading and study. This is an eight-week class designed to facilitate joint Bible study and discussion between mothers and daughters. Each week, we will examine a girl of grace character trait and look to see how women from the Bible modeled these characteristics for us. This includes reading relevant Scripture passages and thinking about how these excerpts from God's Word are relevant for girls today.

Look at the table of contents and briefly touch on the characteristics we will discuss during the course of this study. Moms and daughters may approach weekly study however it fits into their schedules. If they want to read/study a little bit each day, great! If it works better for them to consolidate into two days, excellent! This study is intentionally flexible.

Each week, moms and daughters will also have an optional activity. Encourage class participants to do these activities if at all possible as they relate to each week's theme and will be just plain fun! I am personally a visual learner, so hands-on activities have always helped me wrap my brain around a concept. These weekly activities are age appropriate, fun, and a different approach from traditional study to help moms and their daughters discuss, connect, and learn about Scripture together.

Please make note of a special section for moms in each week's study, called **"From a mommy's heart."** This section is for moms' hearts only and is an opportunity to tie a parent-related topic to each week of study. These sections are designed to complement the discussions moms and daughters are already having and give moms an extra tidbit to reflect on and pray through during their week of study.

girl of grace characteristic:

LOVE

Open each class time with prayer. During your first meeting, take the first ten to fifteen minutes to make introductions. Pick one of the following icebreakers (or use one of your own) to help mothers and daughters get better acquainted.

TOILET PAPER GAME

Take a roll of toilet paper and ask each person how many squares she wants, but don't tell her why. Set a limit from five to ten. Count the number of requested squares, and give them to the class attendee. Repeat until all the participants have the requested amount of toilet paper squares. After everyone has taken her tissue, ask each mom and daughter to share something about herself for every square of toilet paper she has taken.

GOD AND THE FAMILY BOND

Give each mom and daughter a list of questions you have made up ahead of time. Use your imagination to make a list of twenty or more questions like, "Who is your favorite movie star?" or "What is your favorite book?" You can ask about colors, music, plays, TV shows, or hopes for the future. Place two columns next to each of the questions, one for the mother, and one for the daughter. Ask each mom and daughter to write down both her favorite and what she thinks is her mother's or daughter's favorite. The pair goes over the list together. Talk about how God knows us better than even our own family.

aBCS OF Me

First, take a piece of paper and write your name vertically down the left side. Next, choose a word that starts with each letter of your name. The word should describe something about you. Write those words horizontally across the paper, using the letters of your name as the first letter of each descriptive word. After you have listed your words, draw an accompanying picture to illustrate each.

When you are finished, tape your paper to the wall. Ask each mom and daughter to do this on her own. When all posters are complete, have everyone introduce themselves using their name drawing.

eLBOW MatCHarONi

Ask moms and daughters to spread out in the room. Call out things that they have in common, such as "wears same kind of shoes" or "likes the same kind of food." After calling out each characteristic, individuals rush to find as many people as possible with the same thing in common. Attendees with the same characteristic lock elbows and add people until the leader calls time after ten seconds. Disband groups and resume play with a different characteristic. Possible characteristics include birth month, favorite sport, and same middle name.

HUMaN Treasure HUNT

Create a list of fifteen to thirty statements to distribute to the moms and daughters in your class. Give the group a period of time to find people who meet the criteria of different statements on the list. When participants find someone who meets the criteria, they ask that person to sign their list. At the end of the activity, read off the various statements and ask anyone who meets the criteria to stand up.

A sample list may include:

- ♥ Has a blue toothbrush
- ♥ Is an only child
- ♥ Hates chocolate
- ♥ Hasn't got all her second teeth
- ♥ Is having a very happy unbirthday today
- ♥ Can stand on her head and count to ten
- ♥ Knows her ABCs backward

- Has two brothers
- Has green eyes
- Had a shower yesterday

getting Started with *Becoming a girl of grace*

After your class participants have had an opportunity to greet one another, ask moms and daughters to take out their Bibles. Discuss different Bible translations and the benefits of referencing different versions throughout Bible study. If a passage is difficult to understand in one translation, encourage the girls to try another.

Ask someone to read Genesis 1:1–3. Take a few minutes so others can share from different Bible translations they may be using. (It may be helpful for the facilitator to bring two or three different translations to class.)

This exercise is two-fold:
1. It demonstrates a helpful strategy during Bible study when a passage is difficult to understand. Check another translation!
2. This is a great passage to begin *Becoming a Girl of Grace*. This study is based on studying God-breathed Scripture about women who possess character traits that we can and should be applying to our lives today. Genesis 1:1–3 also affirms the power of the spoken word and the power of God's word. He literally spoke our world into being. By studying and understanding Scripture, we are better prepared to defend our faith and spirits from the darkness that dwells among us every day.

preparing for week 1

The first girl of grace characteristic we are going to discuss is love. The first three females we are going to study are Eve, Naomi, and Ruth. Take a few minutes to let class participants share what they know about these fabulous ladies.

After moms and daughters have had an opportunity to share, reiterate that Eve is the first example of a girl of grace that we have. While Adam was formed from the dust of the ground, she was created using one of Adam's ribs. God had a special purpose for her—just as he has a special purpose for every single one of us. Eve was designed to be a helper, a wife, a friend, a mother, a cultivator, a caretaker, an encourager, and a leader.

During study this week, participants will have an opportunity to dig deeper into why Eve was created, why we were created, and what purpose every girl of grace has within the kingdom of God.

Next, we'll take a peek at Naomi and Ruth—one of my favorite stories from the Bible. Talk with moms and daughters in your class about the long, difficult journey that Naomi made. Her life was unimaginably tough! Ask the girls to describe their worst day ever. After they've had a few minutes to share, talk in more detail about Naomi and how sweet Ruth stood beside her in the darkest of times.

One of the words these girls of grace will encounter during their study time this week is "stewardship." Ask the moms and daughters to share what they think stewardship means.

Take a few minutes to let moms and daughters share examples of what stewardship means to them. Here are a few other examples if you need them:

- Pack and distribute meals for your homeless community.

- Collect personal care items and medicines (such as Tylenol, Benadryl, Neosporin, etc.) for your church's mission projects overseas.

- Collect money in a special box to help fund church missions—such as giving money to support missions during VBS week, etc.

- Write thank-you notes to our ministers for their dedication, love, and support.

- Collect school supplies for students in mission schools.

STEWARDSHIP IN ACTION

Take ten to fifteen minutes for a stewardship activity. Pass out note cards and envelopes to each mother/daughter team, and ask them to write a thank-you note to one of the church pastors or staff

> **Stewardship**
> *Merriam Webster*
> *Unabridged Dictionary*
> defines stewardship as:
>
> the individual's responsibility especially in certain religious groups for sharing systematically and proportionately his or her time, talent, and material possessions in the service of God and for the benefit of all humankind

members. Each class participant will write her own note and seal it to be delivered to the church office by the facilitator. Give mom/daughter teams the option to deliver their note cards in person if they like.

TYING IT ALL TOGETHER

All three of the females we will read about this week not only model love for us, but they model stewardship as well. Love and stewardship go hand in hand! God gave Adam and Eve dominion over the earth—which meant caring for the earth and all that's in it. That was our first example of stewardship.

Naomi and Ruth exhibit what it means to love and care for a family member. Love and stewardship are modeled for us by these two women, but in a different way than Eve. Encourage the ladies in your group to think about the similarities and differences between Eve, Naomi, and Ruth as they read and study this week.

Thanksgivings and Prayer Requests

Take the last ten minutes or so of each class to share thanksgivings and prayer requests. These young girls are prayer warriors in training, so keep them in the habit of praying for others and giving thanks when God answers prayers—even if he doesn't answer them the way we thought he would!

girl of grace characteristic:
FaiTH

Open each class time with prayer. After prayer, welcome everyone and take the first few minutes of class for each person to share one blessing she experienced since the last time you were together as a group.

FOLLOW-UP From Week 1: LOVE

Allow some time for mother/daughter teams to share their thoughts and experiences from week 1 of *Becoming a Girl of Grace.*

Some potential questions for discussion:

- ♥ Did you relate to any particular girl of grace role model from week 1? (Eve, Naomi, or Ruth)

- ♥ Do you want to share a little about the connection you felt to this woman from the Bible?

- ♥ What were your thoughts about why God chose to make Eve from one of Adam's ribs instead of from dust like the other animals?

- ♥ What did you think about Naomi and Ruth's story? Did this lead to some good sharing between moms and daughters? Would someone like to share how they were able to relate to Naomi and Ruth's relationship of love and care?

- ♥ How do you girls feel about stewardship after reading and talking through week 1? What does that word mean to you?

- ♥ Did anyone do the "Mommy and Me" activity? How did it go?

Digging into Week 2: Faith

After answering any questions about week 1, direct the discussion to the topic for week 2. The girl of grace characteristic for week 2 is faith. Ask the mom and daughter teams to share what faith means to them. What does that word mean?

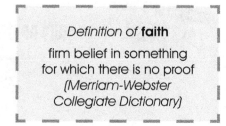

*Definition of **faith***

firm belief in something for which there is no proof *(Merriam-Webster Collegiate Dictionary)*

This week, mom and daughter teams will read about four women of the Bible who model the characteristic of faith for us. They are:

- ♥ Sarah (wife of Abraham);
- ♥ Mary Jesus's (mother);
- ♥ Elizabeth (John the Baptist's mother); and
- ♥ the woman in the crowd.

Ask the girls to share what they remember about these females from the Bible. Moms should join the discussion, too!

Before you get too deep in discussion about the upcoming week's study, take some time to do one or more of the following activities. Explain to participants that these are games that demonstrate the act of faith.

GUESS WHAT?

Assemble participants into a circle in the center of the room. Facilitator will have placed several random and common household items into a brown paper bag. Have the girls and their moms sit in a circle on the floor. The daughters should put blindfolds on and take turns pulling items out of the bag and guessing what they are by feel only. (You could skip the blindfolds and have each girl and each mom reach directly into different bags that you've prepared ahead of time.)

They might know that an apple is an apple, yet they cannot prove it without sight. They simply have faith that they know what they are touching. Likewise, they will know a cotton ball when they feel it because they have had experience with cotton balls in the past and have faith that they are experiencing the same thing. Discuss how our faith in God is much like faith in understanding the items in the bag. While we cannot clearly see God, our experiences with God help us to have faith and identify God's working in our lives.

Faith Trust Walk

Break the class into mom/daughter teams. Give each team a blindfold, and ask the moms to blindfold their daughters first. Once blindfolds are on, the facilitator is going to place obstacles around the room (chairs, items on the floor, etc.). Explain that the object of the game is for moms to lead their daughters from one end of the room to the other using only the sound of their voices. They can walk alongside their daughters and provide directions, but they can't touch them.

Opposing teams can try to mislead the blindfolded member of other teams by giving false directions, but they may be too busy directing their own team member. Then again, the sound of multiple voices may be distraction enough! If one of the girls takes off her blindfold or a mom touches her daughter to direct them, then they are automatically out of the game until the next round.

Direct the moms to turn their blindfolded daughters in a circle two or three times. Then, let them go! Once the round is over, have the moms and daughters switch. It's the moms' turn to be blindfolded! You can repeat the game again if time permits.

After the game, explain that this game is like learning to listen and follow God's voice. Sometimes, you may hear other voices that try to mislead you, but God is always present.

Walking in Faith Isn't Always Easy!

Gather into a circle once more and ask moms and daughters how it felt to walk without feeling in control. Did they feel safe hearing a familiar voice that they knew would lead them to safety? Were the other voices distracting? Talk about why that's like listening to God's voice and how sometimes we have to tune out the distractions around us to hear God.

Ask the group to share an example of a time when they felt like they were taking a step in faith, but they knew God was there and in control.

MUSTARD SEED CRAFT ACTIVITY—IF TIME PERMITS

He replied, "Because you have so little faith. Truly I tell you,
if you have faith as small as a mustard seed, you can say
to this mountain, 'Move from here to there,' and it will move.
Nothing will be impossible for you."

Matthew 17:20

Pick one of the following craft activities:

MUSTARD SEED BOOKMARK

Purchase mustard seeds from the spice aisle. Print the Bible verse Matthew 17:20 (which is about faith as small as a mustard seed) on cardstock, and cut them down to the size of bookmarks you want to use. Every participant (moms and daughters) should get one. Pass out the mustard seeds, and let the girls and moms glue a mustard seed to the bookmark. Crayons and markers may be used to decorate their bookmarks further if they like. Encourage participants to use these bookmarks to mark their places in their Bibles or Bible study books as they read.

MUSTARD SEED NECKLACE

Ahead of time, purchase quarter-sized wooden craft disks and punch a hole in each (using a small drill or awl). Provide ribbons (for the moms and daughters to tie through the hole) along with markers, mustard seeds, and glue. Each participant may decorate her disk and then glue one mustard seed to her necklace. Let each one pick a ribbon to loop through the hole in the disk to complete her necklace. These necklaces will then serve as reminders that just a tiny bit of faith can move mountains.

Thanksgivings and Prayer Requests

Take the last ten minutes or so of class to share thanksgivings and prayer requests. These young girls are prayer warriors in training, so keep them in the habit of praying for others and giving thanks when God answers prayers—even if he doesn't answer them the way we thought he would!

girl of grace characteristic:

WISDOM

Open each class time with prayer. After prayer, welcome everyone and take the first few minutes of class for each person to share one blessing she experienced since the last time you were together as a group.

✤ Follow-up from week 2: faith

Allow some time for mother/daughter teams to share their thoughts and experiences from week 2 of *Becoming a Girl of Grace.*

Some potential questions for discussion:

- ♥ Can anyone remind me again what a nomad is?

- ♥ Did anyone do the "Mommy and Me" activity? What was it like to pitch your tent and then have to move it?

- ♥ What did you pack for your journey? Do you think it would have been tough to live as a nomad like Abraham and Sarah?

- ♥ Sometimes God answers our prayers in unexpected ways—like how God answered Sarah's prayer for a baby. Does someone from the group feel comfortable sharing how God has answered one of your prayers in a way you didn't expect?

- ♥ Faith means believing in something for which there is no proof. The women we read about last week all demonstrated what it means to put their faith into action. To depend on God's timing and trust that he knows what's best isn't always an easy thing to do. Did anyone write your wish or prayers on a piece of paper and prayerfully leave them in your Bible? What did you think about this idea?

⚜ Digging into Week 3: Wisdom

After answering any questions about week 2, direct the discussion to the topic for week 3. The girl of grace characteristic for this week is wisdom. Ask the mom and daughter teams to share what the word "wisdom" means.

During week 3, mom and daughter teams will read about more women of the Bible who model the characteristic of wisdom for us. They are:
- ♥ Miriam (Moses's sister)
- ♥ Deborah
- ♥ Abigail

Ask the girls to share what they remember about these females from the Bible. Moms should join the discussion, too!

Before you get too deep in discussion about the upcoming week's study, take some time to do one or more of the following activities. Explain to participants that these are games that demonstrate the characteristic of wisdom.

CHOICES

Here's what you'll need:
- ♥ three paper bags, a few small plastic bugs, a few small prizes, and marshmallows
- ♥ enough small prizes (pencils, erasers, stickers, etc.) for the number of children in your group, in case they choose the correct bag

With this activity, the goal is to demonstrate that sometimes we make choices for the wrong reasons—and without utilizing prayer and wisdom. Decorate one of the bags so that it's really appealing to the eye. In this bag, you'll slip the small plastic bugs. The next bag should look really unattractive—very plain, dirty, and maybe even torn (but not so kids can see what's inside). Put small prizes in this bag. Leave the third bag plain and unassuming. You can put marshmallows (or any type of small candy) in this bag.

Ask the group which bag they would like to select, and they can only pick one! Once the decision has been made, ask one of the girls to reach into the bag that was chosen. Once they figure out what's inside, talk with the group about what happened. Did they pick the bag that looked the best? When we make choices, we sometimes go with the "best-looking" alternative, but that's not always the best choice. Sometimes, the best choice is the one that looks plain or even worse on the outside. That's why it's important to seek God's wisdom when making important decisions and not rely solely on our own thoughts.

Backpack memory verse activity

Here's what you'll need:

- ♥ backpack or paper sack
- ♥ one item for each word/phrase of the verse, such as basket, water, shawl, small palm-like plant, trail mix, lantern or flashlight, shoes, etc.—you can get creative here. Make it fun!

Print each word or phrase of the verse on a piece of paper and tape each to its corresponding item. Talk about how the women we'll read about this week show great wisdom in their decision-making. They listened to God, and we can also! God's Word is our guide. Explain that the girls and their moms will need to line up single file. When you say go, they'll take turns running to the backpack and pulling out items/words. They may only pull one item out at a time. Each person will place the item/word(s) on the floor. As they pull the items out and display them on the floor, they should work together to put the verse in the correct order.

Suggested verses to use:

- ♥ Exodus 2:3–4: "But when she could hide him no longer, she got a papyrus basket for him and coated it with tar and pitch. Then she placed the child in it and put it among the reeds along the bank of the Nile. His sister stood at a distance to see what would happen to him."

- ♥ Judges 4:4–5 (NLT): "Deborah, the wife of Lappidoth, was a prophet who was judging Israel at that time. She would sit under the Palm of

Deborah, between Ramah and Bethel in the hill country of Ephraim, and the Israelites would go to her for judgment."

♥ Psalm 119:105 (KJV): "Thy word is a lamp unto my feet, and a light unto my path."

Talk for a few minutes about the following:

Why is it important for us to gain knowledge and wisdom? (Discuss ideas.)

Do you have to be an adult to gain wisdom? Why or why not? (Discuss ideas.)

Do you think wisdom is more precious than any earthly treasure? Why or why not? (Discuss ideas.)

Share the following verses:

"Choose my instruction rather than silver,
and knowledge rather than pure gold.
For wisdom is far more valuable than rubies.
Nothing you desire can compare with it.
I, Wisdom, live together with good judgment.
I know where to discover knowledge and discernment."
Proverbs 8:10–12 (NLT):

Treasure Chest

Have the girls and their moms create a treasure chest for the Bible verse above. Every mother/daughter team will need one shoebox or tissue box to transform. They can paint it, attach stickers/foam pieces, or decorate with glitter glue or tissue paper. (Use whatever you have available.) Print copies of the Proverbs verse for each team to put inside their treasure box. Moving forward, each team may use their box as a place to put prayer requests or other Bible verses that speak to their hearts.

Thanksgivings and Prayer Requests

Take the last ten minutes or so of class to share thanksgivings and prayer requests. These young girls are prayer warriors in training, so keep them in the habit of praying for others and giving thanks when God answers prayers—even if he doesn't answer them the way we thought he would!

girl of grace characteristic:

HUMILITY

Open class time with prayer. After prayer, welcome everyone and take the first few minutes of class for each person to share one blessing she experienced since the last time you were together as a group.

Follow-up from Week 3: Wisdom

Allow some time for mother/daughter teams to share their thoughts and experiences from week 3 of *Becoming a Girl of Grace*.

Some potential questions for discussion:

* Which girl of grace from the Bible did you like enjoy reading about the most last week?

* Why do you think you connected with this particular woman from the Bible?

* After going through the last chapter of *Becoming a Girl of Grace*, what does wisdom mean to you now? Is this different from what you thought before you dug a little deeper into the stories of Miriam, Deborah, and Abigail?

* How do you think the outcomes of these women's stories could have differed if they hadn't acted with wisdom?

* Did anyone do the "Mommy and Me" activity? Did anyone bring your compass with you to class?

* Do you know what it means to listen to the voice inside your spirit that guides you in making choices? Can anyone share an example of how listening to your inner compass helped you make a wise choice?

Digging into Week 4: Humility

After answering any questions about week 3, direct the discussion to the topic for week. The girl of grace characteristic for this week is humility. Ask the mom and daughter teams to share what the word "humility" means. Allow for discussion and talk through synonyms of humility— modesty, meekness, humbleness.

> *Definition of* **humility**
>
> Humility (adjectival form: humble) is the quality of being modest and respectful.
>
> *(Wikipedia)*

During week 4, mom and daughter teams will read about two women of the Bible who model the characteristic of humility for us. They are:

* Mary, Jesus's mother
* Rhoda, a servant girl from the New Testament

Ask the girls to share what they remember about these females from the Bible. As always, moms should join the discussion, too!

Take the remaining time to do the following activities. Explain to participants that these are games that demonstrate the characteristic of humility.

a Picture of Humility

Using a large piece of paper (such as a large presentation-style tablet size), ask the girls to help you draw a picture of what humility looks like to them. Let the girls get creative! All you'll need is a large sheet of paper and some markers.

Popcorn Storytelling

Arrange the group into a circle. Explain to the group that all of you are going to tell a "popcorn story." If you have ever done a "popcorn prayer," this is the same concept. Facilitator, you start the story by beginning a tale of a girl who shows humility or humble behavior. You are only going to begin the story and introduce the characters. Each girl and mom will add a detail to the story until it comes back to the facilitator, who wraps up the story on the first round. You can do this activity a few times and give others a turn to begin the story and create new characters. This activity gets the girls' wheels turning about the different ways a person can show humility. Have fun and let the girls use their imagination!

secret HumILITY aGeNTS: week 4 CHaLLeNGe!

Have participants pretend to be "secret humility servants." The first part of this challenge is performing acts of kindness. Ask the girls and moms to perform tasks or do nice things for others without them knowing about it during the upcoming week. The point of the activity is to practice acts of kindness without looking for a reward in return. For example, offer to help siblings with homework or help them with a chore so they can have more free time. Or take a plate of cookies to an elderly neighbor. Even if the girls or moms are recognized for their acts of kindness, the intention is to feel good by serving others.

The second part of this challenge is catching others who serve with humility and thanking them for their thoughtfulness. Give each mom and daughter supplies to make her own "secret humility agent" badge. In addition to their badges, each mom/daughter team will make four special thank-you cards. Ask the teams to deliver these thank-you cards during the next week to individuals they think show acts of humility. These could be their teachers, librarians, janitors, siblings, parents, restaurant workers . . . the sky is the limit! Here's what you'll need:

- white cardstock
- construction paper (all colors)
- markers
- colored pencils
- jewels
- glue
- scissors

Thanksgivings and prayer requests

Take the last ten minutes or so of class to share thanksgivings and prayer requests. These young girls are prayer warriors in training, so keep them in the habit of praying for others and giving thanks when God answers prayers—even if he doesn't answer them the way we thought he would!

girl of grace characteristic:
courage

Open class time with prayer. After prayer, welcome everyone and take the first few minutes of class for each person to share one blessing she experienced since the last time you were together as a group.

✤ FOIIOW-UP From Week 4: Humility

Allow some time for mother/daughter teams to share their thoughts and experiences from week 4 of *Becoming a Girl of Grace.*

Some potential questions for discussion:

* Which girl of grace from the Bible did you most enjoy reading about last week?

* Why do you think you connected with this particular woman from the Bible?

* Last week, some of us were confused about the difference between humility and humiliation. Can someone explain the difference to me now?

* How did your week 4 challenge go? Were our secret humility agents successful in showing others acts of humility?

* Will someone share your experiences as a secret agent with us? Do you think your job as a secret humility agent has made you more aware of the girls of grace characteristic humility?

* Did anyone do the "Mommy and Me" activity? What was that experience like for you girls? Moms? Why do you think this act was so significant when Jesus washed his disciples' feet?

⚜ Digging into Week 5: Courage

After answering any questions about week 4, direct the discussion to the topic for week 5. The girl of grace characteristic for week 5 is courage. Talk about what courage means to the group. Chances are that everyone is familiar with the meaning of courage, but let the girls share their different perspectives.

During week 5, mom and daughter teams will read about two women of the Bible who model the characteristic of courage for us. They are:
* Esther
* Rahab

Ask the girls to share what they remember about these females from the Bible. Does anyone remember that Rahab was Boaz's mother? Since they have studied Ruth, they may find that little tidbit interesting. As always, moms should join the discussion, too!

Take the remaining time to do the following activities. Explain to participants that these are games that demonstrate the characteristic of courage.

Quotes of Courage

Share a quote and correlating picture that reflects the girls of grace characteristic courage. Next, ask mothers and daughters to work in teams and write/illustrate their own quote for courage. Give them a chance to share their vision with the group once everyone is finished.

Materials:

* Large piece of paper (such as a large presentation-style tablet size) for each mother/daughter team
* Markers (enough for each mother/daughter team to create drawings)

On a Roll

Show the girls a piece of copy paper and ask them if there is any way the paper can hold up a book using only one hand to hold the paper. You can ask for several volunteers to try; soon they will realize there is no way. Once you've given a couple of girls the opportunity to try, take the paper and roll it tightly into a tube (with a diameter of about one to one and a half inches). Hold the tube in one hand and carefully place the book on top of one open end of the tube. It should support the book. Practice before your session just in case you have trouble yourself!

Talk with the girls about how the paper represents our ability to show courage. The book represents one of our fears or a scary circumstance. When we try to face it on our own, we fail. We can't face these obstacles alone. However, with God's help and perseverance, we can develop courage to conquer our fears or face challenging situations. With God as our strength and source of courage, we can stand up to the pressure of fear.

Ask the girls to share examples of fears that God can help them conquer: fear of heights, fear of public speaking, fear of spiders, etc.

Materials:

- ♥ one piece of copy paper
- ♥ small book

aCT IT OUT

Split the moms and daughters into small groups to role play situations in which a person shows courage. It's fun to put the girls on one team and moms on another, and then you can switch them out. Draft possible scenarios; print and distribute one to each group. Allow each group to perform its skit for the rest of the class. Depending on your group size, plan for five or six scenarios.

Thanksgivings and prayer requests

Take the last ten minutes or so of class to share thanksgivings and prayer requests. These young girls are prayer warriors in training, so keep them in the habit of praying for others and giving thanks when God answers prayers—even if he doesn't answer them the way we thought he would!

girl of grace characteristic:

WITNESSING
THROUGH a servant's Heart

Open class time with prayer. After prayer, welcome everyone and take the first few minutes of class for each person to share one blessing she experienced since the last time you were together as a group.

Follow-up from week 5: courage

Allow some time for mother/daughter teams to share their thoughts and experiences from week 5 of *Becoming a Girl of Grace*.

Some potential questions for discussion:

- What do you think of Queen Esther's courage after reading and studying her story last week?

- Do you think she showed courage to King Xerxes? Have you ever stood up for someone you felt was being wronged? Has anyone stood up for you in a situation where you felt bullied? What happened?

- The stories we read both reflect turbulent cultures where war was the norm. Thankfully, we don't live in a culture where our cities are in danger of being annihilated, but we do live in a world where we must have courage to stand for our faith. What does this mean to you? Have you ever had to defend your faith? What were the circumstances?

- Sometimes, others perceive Christians as being judgmental instead of kind. Why does it take courage to show others that being a Christian means loving one another?

- Who is the most courageous person you know? Why do you think he or she is courageous? Can you inspire others by your acts of courage? How so?

♥ Did anyone do the "Mommy and Me" activity? What was that experience like for you girls? Moms? Did you have fun?

⚘ Digging into Week 6: Witnessing through a Servant's Heart

After answering any questions about week 5, direct the discussion to the topic for week 6. The girl of grace characteristic for week 6 is witnessing through a servant's heart. Talk about what witnessing means to the group. Now discuss what it means to be a servant, and what it means to be a servant leader. Let the girls share their different perspectives.

During week 6, mom and daughter teams will read about two women of the Bible who show us what it means to witness through a servant's heart.
They are:
♥ Dorcas
♥ Phoebe

Ask the girls to share what they remember about these females from the Bible. They may not be very familiar with these women. Briefly talk about who they are and where you can find their stories.

This week is about witnessing by serving others. Facilitator, identify a service or mission project before class. Arrange the girls and their moms to participate in this project. It could be a project that is sponsored by your church, such as preparing backpacks of food for children or preparing care packages for elderly church members who are homebound. If you are meeting outside of a church setting, investigate a community service project through a local nonprofit organization, such as organizing the pantry at your local food bank or preparing meals for the homeless population in your community.

Spend the remainder of your time working on the service project as a group. Before concluding your time together, remind the girls that they have the power to change another's heart by being a servant leader. They may be young, but God has a special purpose for each girl of grace. Challenge them to seek opportunities in the upcoming week to serve others quietly. Ask them to pray that God will place these ideas on their hearts and use them to show others what a loving and powerful God we serve!

Thanksgivings and Prayer requests

Take the last ten minutes or so of class to share thanksgivings and prayer requests. These young girls are prayer warriors in training, so keep them in the habit of praying for others and giving thanks when God answers prayers—even if he doesn't answer them the way we thought he would!

girl of grace characteristic:

BEING a GODLY LEADER

Open class time with prayer. After prayer, welcome everyone and take the first few minutes of class for each person to share one blessing she experienced since the last time you were together as a group.

FOLLOW-UP FROM WEEK 5: Witnessing through a servant's Heart

Allow some time for mother/daughter teams to share their thoughts and experiences from week 6 of *Becoming a Girl of Grace*.

Some potential questions for discussion:

- ♥ How did everyone like the service project last week?

- ♥ Did anyone do the "Mommy & Me" activity? Who can share the types of volunteer opportunities or service projects they uncovered?

- ♥ We talked a little last week about what it means to be a witness. Dorcas witnessed through her servant's heart by making clothes for the poor in her community. Phoebe was a witness to others through her service to the early church. How do you think your actions reflect your witness to God and the church? Specifically, what actions? Ask for the girls to share.

- ♥ Ask the girls to open their Bibles to Matthew 23:11: "The greatest among you will be your servant." Ask the girls to share what this means to them. Is God asking you to be a slave to your baby brother? Is he asking you to become a housekeeper? How does this passage apply to you?

* In your Heart Check questions for last week, you brainstormed a list with your mom of ways you can serve others.What are some of the things you brainstormed together?

* How does serving others make you feel?

* Why do you think Jesus said it was important to care for those who can't care for themselves?

🌿 Digging into Week 7: Being a godly Leader

After answering any questions about week 6, direct the discussion to the topic for week 7. The girl of grace characteristic for week 7 is being a godly leader. Discuss what it means to be a leader. Ask the girls to describe leader characteristics. Write down what they say. Now ask them to describe a godly leader. Write down those characteristics and discuss any differences. Let the girls share their different perspectives.

During week 7, mom and daughter teams will read about two women of the Bible who show us what it means to be a godly leader. They are:
* Lydia
* Anna

Ask the girls to share what they remember about these females from the Bible. They may not be very familiar with these ladies. Briefly talk about who they are and where you can find their stories.

Take the remaining time to do the following activities.:

rope circles

Prepare four different lengths of rope: twenty feet, fifteen feet, ten feet, and five feet (adjust sizes according to the room you have in your meeting space). Tie each into a circle, put them on the ground, and have all the girls stand inside the big rope. No body part may be outside the rope. Once the girls successfully get into the first rope, ask them to move to the next smaller rope. With each decrease in size, the girls will have to be more creative to fit. They will have to work together. Encourage them to utilize their leadership and teamwork skills.

Materials:
* rope cut into four lengths: twenty, fifteen, ten, and five feet

FOLLOW THE LEADER

Prepare an obstacle course in the room (with chairs, tables, or whatever you have available). Ask the girls and moms to line up single file. Take turns following the leader. Give each girl a turn (and moms, too, if they like). Discuss afterward how the leaders' choices impact a larger group or those who are following them.

FIND THE LEADER

Assemble the moms and daughters into a circle. Ask one of the girls to volunteer to be the "guesser." Once you have your volunteer, send her out of the room so the remaining girls and moms can choose a "leader." Explain to the group that they are to follow the movements of the leader as inconspicuously as they can. They are trying not to make it obvious to the guesser who is the leader.

Ask your guesser to rejoin the room and stand in the middle of the circle. Everyone should begin by swinging their arms back and forth with the leader eventually starting to make additional movements that the group begins to mimic. The girl in the center gets three guesses to find the leader. If time permits, give everyone an opportunity to be the guesser if they would like to.

Talk with the group afterward about how sometimes leading a group can be subtle. Give the girls a chance to share how everyday actions could be copied or mimicked by friends and others they encounter.

Thanksgivings and Prayer Requests

Take the last ten minutes or so of class to share thanksgivings and prayer requests. These young girls are prayer warriors in training, so keep them in the habit of praying for others and giving thanks when God answers prayers—even if he doesn't answer them the way we thought he would!

girl of grace characteristic:
accountability

Open class time with prayer. After prayer, welcome everyone and take the first few minutes of class for each person to share one blessing she experienced since the last time you were together as a group.

Since this is the last week of study, you may want to plan extra time for a celebration unless your group is planning an additional meeting. Celebration activities are included with this week's facilitator's guide.

Follow-Up from Week 5: Being a godly Leader

Allow some time for mother/daughter teams to share their thoughts and experiences from week 7 of *Becoming a Girl of Grace*.

Some potential questions for discussion:

* Let's talk a little about last week's topic. Can anyone share what comes to mind when you think of a godly leader?

* Okay now that we've established what a godly leader is, does anyone want to share who comes to mind when you think of a godly leader?

* What does it mean to lead by example? Why are some of the best leaders those who are willing to set an example for others?

* How can you lead others by example? (Help the girls brainstorm ways to be leaders among their peers and at school.)

* Have you ever made a choice that wasn't popular with your friends, but that you know was a choice that honored God? How did you handle the situation?

* Last week we brainstormed traits of a godly leader. Now, let's talk

about leadership roles that give you an opportunity to serve God. (Remind the girls that they don't have to be adults to be leaders or to make a difference to others.)

Digging into Week 8: accountability

After answering any questions about week 7, direct the discussion to the topic for week 8. The girl of grace characteristic for week 8 is accountability. Explain to the girls that being accountable means taking responsibility for their actions.

This week's study covers the final topic for becoming a girl of grace. Mom and daughter teams will revisit Eve and Miriam as they delve further into what it means to take ownership of our actions. Ask the girls what they remember studying about these ladies. Eve was covered in week one as we discussed the girls of grace characteristic love. Miriam was part of week three's topic, wisdom. If your group will not be meeting another week, spend a little time highlighting how God held both of these women accountable for bad choices.

Take time to discuss how God holds us accountable today. Who else holds us accountable for our actions and choices? Why is it important for us to be held accountable? Let the girls and moms share their thoughts and discuss.

Take the remaining time to do one or more of the following activities.

ASSEMBLY LINE

Arrange chairs into rows of four and ask the girls and moms to sit anywhere they want. Each group of four will be an assembly line. Draw the four steps of the sailboat craft on a board or poster. Explain to the teams that they must work together as part of an assembly line to create the sailboat as quickly as possible.

Give craft supplies to girls sitting on one end of each assembly line and blow a whistle to start the game.

The four steps:

1. The first girl (or mom) must cut out a right triangle from a construction paper sheet.

2. The second girl (or mom) must punch three holes along the long leg of the triangle.

3. The third girl (or mom) must weave a drinking straw through the holes.

4. The fourth girl (or mom) must place a clay ball in the middle of a margarine lid and make the drinking straw stand upright.

The first team to assemble the sailboat craft is the winner. Through this game, the girls will learn the importance of team roles and each individual's accountability within a group.

Materials (each four-person team will need one of each item):

* construction paper

* handheld hole punch

* drinking straws (enough for each team to have one)

* clay balls

* margarine lids (or cardboard circles)

CHOICE & ACCOUNTABILITY

This is an activity that gives the girls a chance to share how they would react in a real-life situation. Before class, draft scenarios that you can share with the girls during Bible study. Here are a few examples to get you started:

* You just found out that saying "Oh my G———" means taking the Lord's name in vain. You've been saying it for years and it's a habit. You've even heard lots of other church members saying it, so maybe it's not that bad. Your school friends will laugh if you start saying "Oh my gosh" instead.

What will you choose to do? What are the consequences of each choice?

* You're the only person you know who doesn't have a Facebook page. Your parents forbid you to get one or even look at other peoples' pages. All your friends are begging you to get one so you can keep in touch online, and they tell you your parents won't find out.

What will you choose to do? What are the consequences of each choice?

♥ You're done with your homework, and it's a beautiful fall day outside. Your brother invites you to go riding bikes with him. You're feeling kind of lazy. "Come on," he says, "It'll be your exercise for the day." You think a good idea would be to exercise your fingers with the TV remote flipping through cartoons instead.

What will you choose to do? What are the consequences of each choice?

BIBLE STUDY MEMENTO

Take time for a group photo. Your last class is a great time to let the girls make a picture frame, ornament, or some other type of craft where you can add a photo. Let the girls decorate their own crafts of choice. Encourage the girls and moms to sign each other's crafts as special mementos from your time together.

Thanksgivings and Prayer requests

Spend the last few minutes of class taking prayer requests and giving thanks that God brought your group together. His plan is perfect, and you are all part of that grand design! Before you go, close in prayer.

❧ about the author

Catherine Bird is an author and speaker who is passionate about moms and tween girls and loves to encourage each—small and tall—in their own journey of faith. In the midst of this crazy thing called life, Catherine simply seeks to glorify God through her family and faith. Through her writing, speaking, and conferences, she encourages moms and tween girls to

- Break out of society's mold of normal and embrace the authentically created girls of grace God designed each of us to be.
- Obliterate the enemy's message that our mommy wisdom is irrelevant for our tween and teen daughters.
- Join the counter culture of other moms and daughters who no longer feel conformed to worldly expectations.
- Find release from busy schedules and be transformed by spending time in God's word together.

As a mom of two daughters, Catherine understands how unique the mother/daughter bond truly is. For the last several years, Catherine has been on an incredible journey to deepen her relationship with her daughters while chasing after God together. Part of this journey led to the birth of Team Grace Ministries (TGM), an organization founded by Catherine with the mission of helping moms and daughters strengthen their relationships through Scripture study and fellowship. The goal of TGM Bible studies and events is that no one remains unchanged, and every mom and daughter leaves with an ignited passion for God and a strengthened bond with one another.

Catherine and her husband currently live near Austin, Texas, with their daughters, one lovable Australian Shepherd, and the quirkiest chocolate Labrador retriever ever. When Catherine is not at her desk writing, she can often be found in Barre class, scoping out some fun new hiking destination with her family, or jumping on the trampoline with her girls. She also believes whole-heartedly in yoga pants, Taco Tuesday, and Aggie football. Catherine holds a bachelor's degree from Texas A&M University.

For the latest updates on future studies, podcasts, and TGM events, visit catherinebird.net.

CPSIA information can be obtained
at www.ICGtesting.com
Printed in the USA
LVOW03s0723070218
565614LV00001B/117/P

9 780891 124153